MAD SHELLEY

MAD SHELLEY

BY
JAMES RAMSEY ULLMAN

GORDIAN PRESS
NEW YORK
1975

Originally Published 1930
Reprinted 1975

Copyright© 1930 by PRINCETON UNIVERSITY PRESS
Renewal Copyright© 1958 by JAMES R. ULLMAN
Published by GORDIAN PRESS, INC.
By Arrangement With
PRINCETON UNIVERSITY PRESS

Library of Congress Cataloging in Publication Data

Ullman, James Ramsey, 1907-1971.
  Mad Shelley.

  Reprint of the 1930 ed. published by the Princeton University Press, Princeton.
  1. Shelley, Percy Bysshe, 1792-1822--Biography--Character. I. Title.
PR5431.U6 1974   821'.7 [B]   74-18406
ISBN 0-87752-178-6

I WISH HERE TO EXPRESS MY GRATEFUL APPRECIATION TO ROBERT E. KAUFMAN, WHOSE UNTIRING WORK AT REVISION AND WHOSE KEEN AND SYMPATHETIC INTEREST HAVE CONTRIBUTED GREATLY TO WHATEVER MERIT THIS LITTLE VOLUME MAY POSSESS.

J.R.U.

A NOTE

The Class of 1909 Prize for the best senior thesis submitted in the Departments of Art and Archaeology, English, Modern Languages and Philosophy in Princeton University was offered in 1929 by an anonymous donor. Each of the four departments concerned selected the two theses which it considered to be the best of those turned in as part of the work of senior year, and the essay here published, Mad Shelley, *was unanimously chosen by the judges as the best of the eight submitted. The Princeton University Press takes pleasure in publishing this essay both as a work of sound literary value and as a striking example of the character of the work now being done by undergraduates in the University.*

CONTENTS

PRESENTATION

	PAGE
Concerning Madness	1
Concerning Shelley	5
Concerning Method	8

PART I: PHENOMENON

The Golden Age	11
Shelley and his Precursors	16
Shelley and his Contemporaries	25
Shelley and his Successors	36
Shelley's Significance	49

PART II: NOUMENON

The Poet's Land	53
The Child	57
Prophet	68
Poet	81
Lover	95

EVALUATION

Unity	109
Direction	113
Mad Shelley	119

PRESENTATION

MATTHEW Arnold relates a story which was told him by a lady who had known Mary Shelley. This lady, it seems, had been asked for advice by the wife of the poet as to a good school where she might send her son, and suggested, reasonably enough, some place where they would teach the boy to think for himself. To which Mrs. Shelley answered: "Teach him to think for himself? Oh, my God, teach him rather to think like other people!"

This from the daughter of William Godwin and Mary Wollstoncraft, who in days past had been, in deed even more than in word, the most militantly and unabashedly radical woman of her nation and her age. This from the wife of Percy Bysshe Shelley. This from Cythna! But then again, perhaps it is not so strange that she who had been the bride and the beloved of the maddest of men should in the afternoon of her life desire that her child, above all things, should be normal and tractable—and sane.

Concerning Madness

The heavens may be inscrutable, the ceiling of the sky may be remote, and those who keep their court beyond its arching, star-paved sweep may be forever silent and aloof; life may be a dream, life may be insanity or illusion or nonentity, life, as a matter of fact, may be almost any old thing, and cosmic riddles may wail their souls away for attention and respect: men have other things to attend to. Pleasurable things. Important things. For must we not have decently cooked food to eat and reasonably soft beds on which to sleep and tolerably dull friends with whom we may innocuously and soothingly pass the time of day? Must we not have "things to do" to keep us busy? and "law and order" to insure our comparative safety when we walk out on a dark night with a hundred dollars in our pocket? and the traditions and institutions of society to overawe us with their vast and incontrovertible assurance of system and security? Over and above all things we demand that life be reasonable and orderly and sane; if there are no basic, rock-ribbed verities in the scheme of things, lo! we will create them to our needs, and if there remain unanswered questions, surely it will profit us little to concern ourselves with them. We are creatures of earth, and to earth we bend our eyes, crying that it is a good earth and a reliable, reasonable, comfortable earth. We desire it so; hence it is so. We would be content; hence we are content. We would be sane; hence we are sane. And we fear the madman.

Plato, rich in years and in the accumulated wisdom of a great civilization, was, for all his idealistic abstractions of form and essence, very much of a pragmatist and a humanist, and in the formulation of his utopian Republic he is fully aware of the dangers of that demi-world of twilit ambiguity which lies forever just beyond the bounds of acceptance and the rational life. He knows that men who have tasted eternity will look cavalierly upon the temporal world and that those who in spirit have sat like Tantalus at the table of the gods will look with none too hearty reverence upon the guardians of even the most reputable commonwealth. Hence, such as these are to be banished from his "almost perfect State," lest their vague and vain imaginings weaken the strong foundations of reason and empiric morality upon which his edifice is raised. He knew, indeed, that there are ascending levels of sanity, just as there are of wisdom, and he knew that the world would not be rational and reasonable in the same way to the meanest artisan and the philosopher-king. But reasonable and rational it must be to all. In his clear Greek mind, untroubled by the shrieking self-assertiveness of unborn Fausts to come, this truest Hellene of them all saw man as a primarily social creature, and therefore man's chief concern was to live "justly" with his fellows. To this end reason was his greatest friend, and, conversely, all that was opposed to reason was his most dangerous foe. And worst of all was madness.

Plato's world was a static one; he lacked the Heraclitan sense of flux and change, and in his conscious philosophic mind he approached the unconscious bourgeois mind in his desire for conformity and uniformity. In the finely woven texture of his state the ravings of the less-than-sane were no more dangerous than the ravings of the more-than-sane; hence seer and singer and passionate lover were to be banished as summarily as Tom o'-Bedlam. They, above all others, were subject to the wildest aberrations from rational life and thought, and, in their furious, unpredictable counter charges against the established current of life, were most likely to disrupt society. Poet, prophet, and lover—the maddest of men, as Plato saw them: drunker than Silenus on the wooded slopes of Cynthus, inspired with the surmise and the vision of an undreamed glory, and amuck in a well fed, well ordered world in which men's dearest wish is to be left undisturbed. Society, if left at the mercies of such as these, would soon be reduced to chaos: so argued Plato, himself a poet in words, if not in spirit, and so have the great masses of the afterworld, in their own inarticulately subconscious way, argued too. Judged by the standards of the diffuse many, the poet, the prophet, and the lover are monomaniacs; judged by any standards they are lonely and strange and absorbed. They raise their eyes to another heaven than ours; they do homage to another God than ours; they see a gleam where we see night and fog, and they tumble into ditches which we take at a stride. They scorn our aims and goals and know not their own; they are dissatisfied when we are content, austere when we are comfortable, raging when we are at peace; they are straight, unwavering lines in a world of gentle curves and aimless angles. In brief, they are different.

It is an aged but unrusted platitude that "difference" is the cardinal sin. Prophets and poets and storming lovers are all very well when viewed from a safe perspective of place or time, and—for the very reason of their difference—are apt to furnish many pleasantly thrilling hours in the library; but in the reality of their living presence the world has found them otherwise. No one—and with good reason—wants Cassandra for a sister, Dante for a playfellow, or Romeo for a roommate. In their proper settings they are fascinating, much as are Alpine peaks or television or the canals of Mars; at a proper distance we can perceive that they are beautiful, but when we approach more closely we see too that they are mad. Madmen are apt to be a menace and they are dead certain to be a strain. The world knows this when with clumsy intuition it opposes its massed earthliness to the soaring spirits of its rarest children; Plato knew it when he banished the poet, the prophet, and the lover from the confines of his ordered commonwealth; and Mary Shelley knew it when she cast about for a good school in which her boy might be moulded

PRESENTATION

into an Englishman, a gentleman, and a mediocrity. Perhaps she knew it best of all.

Concerning Shelley

Shelley was mad. In a society in which conformity is the beginning and the end of sanity the fact is incontrovertible. It is easy enough for the casual critic of today, when a century has passed since the white-hot flame of the living man was extinguished in the waters of the Bay of Spezzia and when time has effected her clarifying necromancy, to hail him as an image and a symbol and to forget that behind this mysterious perfection of the eternal Shelley there is the spirit of another temporal Shelley who dwelt upon the earth and moved among other men and who, by some few of them, was considered not quite so perfect. Time clarifies, but it also effaces; the uprolling years, which bring into focus the ultimate value of men and events serve no less to obscure the smaller, human things of days gone by. It is fine enough to hold a well typed, inoffensive book upon one's knees and swing for a brief hour into the gaudy dreamworlds which the sad, bad, glad, mad spirits of the past have wrought; they exist to entertain and to exalt us upon demand, and when the dinner-bell rings and they are no longer wanted, they may safely be relegated to the orderly limbo of the shelf. Homer may have been a drunkard, Coleridge a dope-fiend, Villon a sneak-thief and a whoremaster, Bacon a defrauder, Von Platen a pervert, indeed the whole galaxy of the long-dead great may, for all we care, have been in their day the most dangerous and reprehensible of men; what matters to us is that they created beauty. Their contemporaries thought differently, and those of us who are unfortunate enough to have a bona-fide, not at all dead poet, prophet, or passionate lover

MAD SHELLEY

in our immediate circle are apt to think differently too. Genius is the present's blessing to eternity, but it is also eternity's curse to the present.

The evaluation of a man depends upon the perspective in which he stands. The Shelley of today and tomorrow and a thousand years from tomorrow, while he may very well be different from other men and, therefore, in the myopic eyes of his contemporaries, a bit mad, is unfadingly beautiful. That is the important thing to *us*. The Shelley of a century ago—the waking, breathing, living man—while he may very well have created verses and dreamed dreams of surpassing ideal beauty, was without doubt dangerously mad—a misfit, a trouble-maker, and a menace to organized society. That was the important thing to *his* age. And let us not forget that if he lived today among us we would feel the same. We too, with the great massed sanity of numbers, would cry out that, while ideally it is all very well for dear posterity to be vouchsafed a legacy of sublime thought and song, it is far from well for a militant maniac to be allowed at large, whose whole soul is dedicated to the overthrow of that world and those principles which we hold most dear. Shelley today would have been a Communist. He would have constructed a new "Laon and Cythna" from the shades of Sacco and Vanzetti. As it is, he may very well be Alvin Fuller's favorite poet.

To his contemporaries—and in this respect his contemporaries might just as well have been men of the Greece of Pericles or the medieval world of the Inquisition or the America of Henry Ford—Shelley was a strange and alien being, a cross-scarping on the Rock of Ages. Shelley was mad. The healthily thick-witted young Britishers of Eton knew it with the canny wisdom of boyhood from the first

PRESENTATION

moment when the incredible creature appeared in their midst; Timothy Shelley knew it when, after the débâcle of Oxford, he visited his son and the Aristophanic Hogg in their London lodgings; Elizabeth Hitchener knew it in the empty afterdays of her "Brown Demonship"; Harriet Westbrook knew it when, broken and diseased, she stood in the last moment of her life on the bank of the Serpentine and thought for a final instant of the pure and incredibly noble wretch who had brought her to this end. Even those wiser, deeper men and women who knew and loved him and in a measure understood him could not but look upon Shelley as a being essentially different from themselves and from all men. To such worthy citizens of the world as Hogg, Peacock, Leigh Hunt, and Trelawney he was a never failing fountain of mystery and wonder, and in the memoirs which they have left of him, however dissimilar may be their attitudes and reactions, the omnipresent touchstone to the character of the poet is his "difference." Is it, indeed, not peculiarly significant that such a wholly unliterary globe-trotter as Trelawney should even have been moved to write of him at all? No one who ever came to know Shelley escaped the sensation—no, the conviction—that he was built of another fabric and animated by another breath than common men. Even the cynical worldling, Byron, as reft of faith and illusion as Mephistopheles himself, was always aware that in his presence there was awe and wonder; and it was no casual encomium on the dead when this man, who believed in nothing and loved nothing, could say of Shelley: "He was without exception the best and least selfish man I ever knew." And the last word is Mary Shelley's, the best of wives and perhaps the only woman in England who could have lived with the poet steadily and stood the pace, when she looked about for a school for her son. She knew that "difference" was madness, and she knew the price. It was too much.

We think otherwise.

Concerning Method

Shelley, for better or worse, was more than a poet. He was possessed, in a more spectacularly intense degree than any other man of whom history tells us, of that triplicate madness of which Plato speaks: he is singer, seer, lover; he is all three of them fused together; and in him, as in no other man, they become one. In his conscious mind he was a thinker and a philosopher, and, to some extent, a follower of that very Plato who would have banished him with horror from his well-ordered commonwealth; but once his ideas had taken root within him and the pointing hand of thought had indicated the way, the Eumenides themselves would sooner have wavered from their path than Shelley from his. "I go forward until I am stopped, but I never am stopped." This from the most genuinely modest of men. We shall seek later to look deeper into this astounding truth, for it explains much of his nature. In a world of confusion, and cross-purposes, and ambiguities the process has the simplicity of insanity. To borrow a phrase from Ibsen, "People don't do such things." But Shelley did.

This is not the place, in the first presentation of the man, to attempt a generalization or an evaluation. One fact, however, must be made clear: whether happily or unhappily, for good or for evil, as a challenge or as a warning to men, Shelley was unique. Both to his contemporaries, who saw him as a man and an individual, and to the afterworld, who see him as a symbol and a milestone in the

PRESENTATION

sweep of civilization, he has stood forth as an isolated phenomenon among men, a being so aflame with visions of which the mass of men have not the least surmise, that he appears alternately more and less than human—wholly human, never. He is unique, not so much in what he thinks as in how he thinks, and, most of all, in what he *is*. We have postulated that he is different; hence that, to the extent to which he is different, he is mad. We must seek to find in this strange jumble of madness and beauty some touchstone whereby we may understand the man as a whole and as he really was—not, on the one hand, the time-washed, apotheosized singer of surpassing verse, nor on the other, the bad-boy of Regency England; not the pure, etherealized spirit which the twentieth century recognizes in "Adonais" and "Prometheus" and the "Indian Serenade," nor yet the calloused demon who, absorbed in his rainbow dreams of the cosmos, could hear of Harriet Westbrook's suicide and speak not a word. Somewhere at the core of all these facets which Shelley offers to the world there is something whole and unified and incredibly simple, so whole in itself that it is almost incomprehensible, so unified that it is unparalleled in our experience or imaginings, so simple that it is mad. That is the Shelley whom (doubtless with unwarranted presumption) we seek.

It has been indicated that the approaches to Shelley are two in number: to borrow a perhaps ponderous, but nevertheless inescapable, expression from Kant, we must see him either as a phenomenon or as a noumenon; that is, we must consider him either as a part of a whole or as a whole in itself. To deal with a phenomenon is primarily to give it its place in the larger scheme of things and to point its relationships, both in time and in space, to other phenomena; in dealing with a noumenon, on the other hand, the concern is with the thing in itself. In our quest for the most nearly accurate conception of what Shelley is we shall proceed along these two lines. In the first part (Phenomenon) he will be examined as objectively as possible, and from the vantage ground of the twentieth century we shall attempt to place him, historically and symbolically, in his proper position in the world of which he was a part. And in the second part (Noumenon) we shall seek to forget all background and relationship and causality and to see him, subjectively if we can, as a man and an individual—complete in himself. By traversing these two different roads, which yet have their ending on the entity we seek, we may perhaps be able to see Shelley in his varied aspects, as image and as man, as dead poet and living misfit, as a part of a whole and as a whole in himself,— and thus in the end to see *him*. In the beginning we are certain of but one thing: that he is not as other men. Why?

PART I

PHENOMENON

The Golden Age

IT WILL contradict neither the Spenglerites nor the more melioristic historians to assert that the western world has known three Golden Ages of the spirit. The first of these was in Periclean Greece, the second in the High Renaissance, and the third—so close to us yet that its form and spirit are at best seen but vaguely and turbidly—in the era of the French Revolution. Each of these high noons of civilization was, of course, in many respects vastly different from the others: each had its own culture and tradition behind it and each was fostered and brought to fruition by peoples whose natures as well as whose backgrounds were vastly dissimilar. The Greece of Plato and Aristotle, of Sophocles and Praxiteles, of Pericles and Alexander, took root in the primitive morning-world of the old Aegean civilization and developed through the centuries of the city-states to the glory of its prime; the wave that at its crest produced Leonardo, Michaelangelo, Luther, Erasmus, and Shakespeare had its beginning in the sombre, scholastic world of the Middle Ages; and the final flowering of the last century, the day of Kant and Beethoven and Napoleon and Goethe and Shelley, had its seed-time in the tortuous, musty-mouthed rationalism of the seventeenth and eighteenth centuries. Each of these Ages was different from the others; each built upon its predecessors and each expressed its own peculiar spirit in its own peculiar way. But this they had in common: they were all of them periods in which the spirit of man was most free, and the song and thought of man was most noble; they were all Golden.

By the latter half of the eighteenth century western Europe had grown up. Even as Greece twenty-three hundred years before had attained through the sweat of centuries to the strong maturity of the day of Salamis and Marathon, even as Rome had struggled upon the backs of its heroes and its legions to the ultimate florid splendor of the Empire, so had England at long last apparently "arrived." Behind now lay the vague, shadow-hemmed centuries of the Middle Ages; behind lay the birth-pangs of the Renaissance and the unbridled, star-aspiring spirit of the new-born; behind lay the silly yet portentous days of seventeenth century adolescence with its extremes of Puritan morality and Restoration devilishness; behind, indeed, lay the whole long and craggy ascent from barbarism and nonentity, and the sunlit upland had been reached. Hard-boiled and wise in the ways of the world, Britannia sprawled out gargantuan limbs, surveyed the scene, and approved its attainments. The Hanoverians lolled comfortably on a well upholstered throne; society moved decorously through resplendent ballrooms, went in for culture in a mild, digestible way, and swathed itself in a pleasing cloak of sophistication; the rich had ease and luxury, and the masses occupation and amusement; the government was stable, God was presumably in His heaven, and life moved along unobtrusively in deep and well oiled grooves. The old order had reached its zenith, and there being no more perceptible worlds to conquer, it was content with itself, shrugged a wise and indifferent shoulder at things unknown, and asked few questions.

PHENOMENON

England was fat, comfortable, and middle-aged. It was ripe for a fall.

Few truisms are more reliable than that every movement begets its countermovement and every age its malcontents. For a long time now, upon the well ordered stage of eighteenth century Europe, new and ominous omens had been abroad; there was thunder on the left and it was rapidly pealing up and over toward the meridian. Voltaire and Swift and Fielding had long since flung forth their invective and their laughter at plump and periwigged complacency, and everywhere were new, audacious spirits who joyed to turn their sturdy rationalism inward and watch it eat itself away. The worldlings, true children of their century, dipped their pens in gall, and in bitterest denunciation and satire inveighed against those manners and traditions to which they themselves still played the ape. The age was turning against itself, and if at first it had, perforce, to use the weapons of its enemy, the change was soon to come. In England a new class of poets was arising, sensitive and uncalloused men who fled the blatant, hard-eyed civilization of the cities and found in the shelter of the country-side solace and inspiration. Imitating Pope was no longer the beginning and the end of art; new poets were doing homage to new gods. Thomson, Collins, Gray, Percy, Chatterton, Cowper, Burns, Blake—theirs was yet, perhaps, a wan and undeveloped romanticism, but it bore marvellous fruit.

But in the world of men and deeds there was also change and disquiet, and, beyond the confines of England, in every country of the western world, men and peoples were imperceptibly uprooting themselves from the sterile soil of an outworn past. Across the Atlantic unheard-of ideas and ideals were being forged into realities with unprecedented audacity; from out of Friedrich's frenchified Germany reverberated the strident, hysterical discords of the "Sturm und Drang"; and from the shores of Lake Geneva there poured down upon Europe the unending and unquenchable words of an unhappy prophet. A new order of pamphleteers and radicals—Helvetius, Holbach, Condorcet, Tom Paine, Holcroft, Godwin—men of passionate conviction and unwavering zeal, had arisen and were preaching a new gospel; from the seclusion of studies and laboratories wise men with cold eyes were composedly making unbelievable announcements and proclaiming the black magic of science; and from alleyway and vineyard of France arose pregnant and disturbing mutterings. On every prophet's lip the shibboleth was "Freedom." From before the eyes of a well ordered and reluctant England horizons were receding, and beneath well planted feet the reliable, ageless earth began to swell. France fermented, boiled, and at last exploded. On the twentieth of June, 1789, a hobbledehoy mob met on a tennis court in Paris; twenty days later the world was upside down.

Solid England looked and felt and rocked to its base. A few short miles away across the Channel the gilt and marble edifice of the Bourbons shivered feebly and collapsed into a welter of blood, and triumphant upon its ruins, with bloodshot eyes and singing heart, stood the peasant of France, ignorant and inspired, louse-ridden and exalted, shouting magnificently of "liberté, égalité, et fraternité" as he rolled in the mud and grinned to the thud of the guillotine. The world, and in particular that spot in the world which a few short years before had seemed the very fulcrum of the sturdy western civilization, was in chaos, and even the most beetle-browed of Oxford dons and the most apple-cheeked of Derbyshire squires could not but feel some vagrant breath of the typhoon. Clerk and philosopher, banker and huckster, dragoon and aesthete, each in his own way was forced to consider the spectacle and to catch, in whatever perspective, some fleeting glimpse of what was happening, to accept or dismiss, to approve, palliate, or condemn. The masses, naturally enough, condemned. Close to the earth and stirred by imminent realities, they found in the fine, high frenzy of the time only carnage and horror and disruption. They could not see the splendor of the Revolution, for the red gutters of Paris; the greatness of Napoleon, for the corpse-strewn fields of Austerlitz, Jena and Waterloo; the stature of Goethe, for the agonies of heel-tramped Germany. The fact, in its awful, threatening nearness, obscured the spirit, and in the inextricable madness of the Here and Now men were blinded to the magnificence of "The Idea."

Even the higher, deeper spirits of the age—the poets and thinkers of England who themselves were children of the upheaval and precursors of the new order—were compelled to haul in their idealistic sails before the storm of actuality. Wordsworth and Coleridge, profound and earnest men, turned in the end with loathing from the revolution which in its first, high-hearted outburst they had hailed as the dawn of a new and radiant day and which before their eyes had turned the earth into an abattoir. It was too much—too much even in sweet Freedom's name. The game was not worth the candle, and a dubious emancipation of the spirit was small compensation for the insecurity and misery to which living men were subjected. They were too closely caught up in the crazy-quilt themselves to perceive that those very things against which they cried out were destined in days to come to be the eternal milestones of their era, and that the spirit which in its one manifestation was responsible for so much of butchery and inhumanity was in its other the wellspring of the thought and song that was the bright, particular glory of this greatest Golden Age. Or, if they did perceive, they did not care. The massed, human sanity of the earth arose and demanded that this madness cease.

Three men stood apart—the three greatest. Goethe, wisest of all, smiled down from Olympian serenity at the foolish little men with their foolish little troubles, and builded for eternity. Napoleon, "fateful executor of a command unknown," played ball with civilization and, in his unswerving, meteoric flight across the scene, furnished the ultimate incarnation of that "world-madness" which for a brief watch had thrilled Europe with a wild surmise and of which a mangled world was now heartily sick. And in England there was another madman—a slim, childlike, singing madman—who alone of all his countrymen kept faith to the end in the "Cause," who saw beyond the substance to the spirit, and who in the face of a world in which there appeared to be neither reason nor hope nor humanity nor peace for men still raised his prophet's cry against the sun—and believed—and affirmed. That was Shelley.

Shelley and his Precursors

During the latter half of the eighteenth century there were two large and fairly discrete streams in European thought and literature. The most deeply rooted and permeating of these was the humanitarian rationalism which had sprung into being as a more or less conscious reaction to the barbaric extravaganzas of the Renaissance and which, in the course of some two centuries, had gained almost universal acceptance in the intellectual world. The second stream, which did not rise to the surface until along about the middle of the eighteenth century and which, however influential in some respects, never attained to more than second-fiddleship, may best be called pseudo-romanticism. For an understanding of that amazing spree of the spirit with which both England and the other great nations of Europe hailed the birth of the nineteenth century, an examination of these streams is very helpful; for an understanding of Shelley—wildest of individualists, but at the same time the most perfect child of his age—it is indispensable. By sketching these two courses of thought and, insofar as possible, correlating them with the poet's reading and thinking we shall try to determine Shelley's spiritual ancestors.

Classical learning and literature reached England in the full tide of the Renaissance and immediately became part and parcel of British thought. During the brief, high-spirited reign of Shakespeare and the Elizabethan crew of roughneck geniuses, its influence was felt more as a half-hidden restraining power than as an outright model and formula—more, one may say, as form than as spirit; but with the passing of the years it again assumed ascendency in the guise of the noted and notorious neo-classicism which held the spirit of literature in its vise for the century between 1650 and 1750. From the death of Milton to the publication of the "Lyrical Ballads" of Wordsworth and Coleridge, there was in the English language no true, singing poet of the first rank. "Singing" is said advisedly, for Donne, Dryden and Pope were all admirable poets in their own way. But that way was limited; in an age which worshipped at the shrine of common sense and mannered regularity in all things, the high, tameless beauty of free, spontaneous song was both impossible and, to them, undesirable. "The world was too much with them," and poetry, which of all forms of expression must be least circumscribed and shackled, was held close to earth. It was an age of prose, social-mindedness, and reason—the age of Voltaire and Newton and Adam Smith and Swift, Fielding and Lessing and Samuel Johnson, great thinkers all, and in their various fields the moulders of human thought for centuries to come, but men whose approach to life was the very opposite of poetic. Rationalism and pseudo-classicism stifled the delicate Muses, but in the hands of the novelists, scientists and social thinkers they became the secure groundwork for that healthy humanitarianism which was the contribution and the glory of the eighteenth century. It was this reasoned, earthly attitude toward life, at the first glance so completely opposite to the rhapsodical spirit of lyric poetry, that furnished the background and the initial promises for the supreme singers of the third Golden Age. It was upon the solid rock of prosaic, empiric thought that Shelley reared his edifice of dreams and starlight.

Mrs. Shelley tells us in her memoirs that the poet in his conscious mind was never quite certain whether he was primarily a singer or a metaphysician. Posterity, prizing living beauty above dubious truth, has answered the question for him; but the important fact remains, and must not be undervalued, that Shelley always *began* his flights from the rock-bottom of rational thought and that, in his attitude to life, he is more of a systematic philosopher than any other English poet. As such, he stands in close relation to the thinkers of the preceding century—to Locke, Hume, and Kant, whom he read and studied carefully, and especially to Bishop Berkeley, whose idealism he in a great measure accepted and transmuted into the stuff of his lyric dreams.

"Nought is but that which feels itself to be."

Thus speaks Ahasuerus in "Hellas." And elsewhere, too, in Shelley we meet often with the Berkeleyan assertion that it is consciousness and not external nature which is the true reality. But his mind was too alive and too powerfully individualistic to accept ready-made anyone's theory of the universe; he borrowed from earlier thinkers but he did not accept any of them outright.

The influence of the less abstract and more social philosophers he felt more strongly; indeed, in the early years of "The Necessity of Atheism," "The Declaration of Rights," and other immature political outbursts, he was little more than a self-appointed mouthpiece for William Godwin. Godwin himself was by no means the original fountain-head from which flowed the revolutionary theories of the time. As the eighteenth century progressed, the humanitarianism of the age, which in the beginning had found expression chiefly in satire and invective, tended ever more and more toward downright radical propaganda against the current "tempora et mores." The worldly mockery of Voltaire, Swift, and Fielding had given place to the more dangerous, if infinitely less artistic, purposefulness of a new generation of malcontents. Everywhere, and especially in France, that most social-minded of all nations, these men were inveighing against the existing order of things and sowing the seed of revolution. Helvetius, Holbach, Condorcet, and the great Rousseau wrote with the impassioned zeal of prophecy and kept out of prison as best they could; in England their doctrines were promulgated by Godwin, Tom Paine, and such lesser lights as Volney and Holcroft. These men—with the definite exception of Jean-Jacques and the possible exception of Paine—had broken with the old tradition of "literary reform." They were the "Reds" of their day; with them the "Cause" came first, last, and all the time. And their cause was Freedom.

It was in this school of radical humanitarianism that Shelley's social thinking developed. Before he was twenty-one he had read and—need one add—absorbed the writings of the "Encyclopedists." He knew Helvetius' "Essais sur L'Esprit," Holbach's "Système de Nature," and the "Nouvelle Héloïse" and "Contrat Social" of Rousseau; as early as his Eton days, Dowden tells us, he dreamed with Condorcet of the endless progress of the race and of human perfectibility. And superimposed upon all these was the famous "Political Justice" of Godwin, in the pages of which he found a well-nigh perfect expression of those ideas and ideals with which his soul was already aflame. The influence of this treatise on Shelley has doubtless been overemphasized, for he, of all men, was the last to accept the hand-me-down theories of others; but that it did affect him deeply is undeniable, especially in his early, uncritical days when the immediate questions of social revolution were the almost exclusive vortex of his thought. As he matured, he outgrew all the thinkers who had contributed to his novitiate. Materialism did not clip his wings for long, and he soon lost that childishly defiant hatred of all religion which he had sucked from the teachings of the great French radicals. But in his affiliations as well as in his militant individualism, he was a true child of the Revolution and of the earnest, rationalistic thinkers of an earlier generation who had given it its premises and its direction. He shared not only their emotional enthusiasm, but he was also in intellectual accord with their basic dogmas and beliefs; and even in the later, riper days of golden song, when as a spirit pure and free and disembodied he soared so far above the toiling world of transient men and transient things, he retained that credo of social reform and that unwavering belief in the perfectibility of man which had been born of the reasoning humanitarianism of the eighteenth century. No men and no schools can be said to have formed Shelley; what they did was to reinforce his beliefs and supply food for his insatiable mind. As a poet he must make his bow to God alone; but as a thinker and philosopher of the Revolution —in many respects the most sublime thinker which that world-madness produced—he is the lineal descendant of those prosaic, earthly reasoners of an earlier generation whose spirit and whose attitude toward life seem at first glance to be so diametrically opposed to his.

In the second half of the eighteenth century there arose from the main current of rationalism and realism a stream of literary thought which we have already referred to as having left its mark on Shelley. This was the pseudo-romantic outburst, which for a considerable time attained a great vogue throughout the length and breadth of Europe and which displayed itself in such various manifestations as medievalism, Rosicrucianism, the Gothic novel, and the Byronic hero. It was a weird and not seldom ridiculous spree of the imagination—an understandable reaction to the common sense and sophistication of the times—and should not be confused with the genuine romantic soul-stirrings of such men as Thomson, Gray, Cowper and Burns. Whereas the art of these true precursors of Wordsworth and Coleridge tended ever toward simplicity and naturalness, the pseudo-romanticism of the time took precisely the opposite course toward exuberant fancy and grotesquerie. The whole effect was what might be expected from a portly and middle-aged gentleman, who, rather weary of respectability, has decided to have a fling. The artificiality of the reaction was even greater than that of the militant worldliness in which it engendered. In England it had its source in the "sensibility-sentimentality" school of behavior, according to the tenets of which a person of fashion was occasionally to indulge himself in a gamut of the less violent emotions; and its high-priest was Lawrence Sterne. The Gothic novel, with its attendant conglomeration of pure maidens, indescribably villainous villains, and elaborate supernatural machinery, was introduced by Horace Walpole, himself—significantly enough—a typical worldly lordling of the old régime, and at once proved to be sure-fire stuff. This type of story reached the height of its popularity in the closing decade of the century, when all England shuddered to the extravaganzas of Clara Reeve, Ann Radcliffe and Monk Lewis. Even Walter Scott was drawn into the current; in Germany the leading sponsor of the horror-motif was E. T. A. Hoffmann, in America Edgar Allan Poe.

It is small wonder that this universal vogue worked its effect upon so omnivorous a reader as Shelley. From his earliest childhood he had a passion for strange and occult things; at Field Place he delighted in terrifying his younger sisters with concocted tales of mystery and horror; at Eton he played alchemist and Rosicrucian and on one occasion was interrupted by his housemaster, Bethel, in the very act of "calling up the devil." He read the Gothic romances voraciously—especially those of the then celebrated Monk Lewis—and, under their compelling influence, delivered himself of "Zastrozzi" and "St. Irvyne, or the Rosicrucian" at the respective ages of seventeen and eighteen. On the surface these two efforts are perhaps as awful tripe as adolescent genius has ever produced; whole sections are transplanted bodily from Lewis, and Shelley's own contributions are even more wildly ridiculous than those of his master. Even in his later, wiser days the spell remained, and the story is well known of how, during their days together on the shores of Lake Geneva, he and Byron, Mary and Claire Clairmont passed away the evenings in the mingled pleasure and horror of fabricating ghost stories. His nerves were as fine as a thread of silk, as taut as a bow-string, and his mind as delicately susceptible to all impressions as a seismograph. Polidori, a member of the Geneva circle, writes in his diary that on one occasion, when ghosts and demons were running wild, Shelley was looking at his wife and suddenly thought of a woman he had heard of who had eyes instead of nipples. He, "suddenly shrieking and putting his hands to his head, ran out of the room with a candle." The grotesque image was too much for his inflammable brain. But the mystical and supernatural fascinated even more than it terrified him; he talked constantly with Byron of the artificial creation of life and the possibilities of galvanism, and he was extremely interested in the development of Mary's story of "Frankenstein," perhaps the greatest of Gothic novels, on which she worked in Switzerland. Never could he shake off his almost morbid susceptibility to the ghostly and horrible which Monk Lewis and his grisly crew had early implanted in his hypersensitive mind.

But it is surely neither fair nor correct to assert, as Jeaffreson, that most petty and falsifying of biographers, has done, that the influence of flamboyant-romantic literature on Shelley was all for the bad. "Zastrozzi" and "St. Irvyne" are admittedly pretty terrible stuff—even from a schoolboy; but a closer observation and more subtle appreciation will unearth even in these monstrosities of adolescent fancy hints and surmises of that incomparably powerful imagination and that unshakable faith in the innate goodness and greatness of man which, in their purer, higher development, were later to be the glory of the poet's song. From the very cradle his mind was aflame; and before age and wisdom came to mature it with their leaven of sober thought, it was inevitable that it burst forth now and again in weird and horrid forms. And through his later life, too, as has been indicated above, this most extraordinary of all children still knew the child's fearful fascination for things unknown: he had trances, visions; he saw images of the most appalling horror and dreamed dreams of unspeakable things. But let it not be forgotten that his over-developed and often feverishly unhealthy imagination which, in one manifestation, resulted in hideousness and terror was the very same living force which, in another, was the spring from which flowed the splendors of "Prometheus" and the mystical magic of "Adonais." Dr. Johnson has spoken of "the dangerous prevalence of the imagination," and warned against its malignant powers. Shelley was imagination incarnate; and he had to pay the price. That that price was not greater is the highest tribute to his magnificent intellectual power and to the solidity of his thought. It would have been not only easy but almost natural for a man with so sensitive a mind to have flown off the handle altogether, as did Novalis and Brentano, Hölderlin and Kleist, and so many other of the morbidly anti-intellectual Germans of the time. He did not do so, because in him mind and spirit, thought and feeling mingled and were inextricably one. Shelley was no more formed imaginatively by the "baroque-romantic" school than he was formed intellectually by the stronger, deeper current of rational humanitarianism. His spirit and his mind, we repeat and cannot repeat too often, were his own, and what he owes to his precursors is not the structure, but the foundation and reinforcement of his ideas and ideals. They were the soil from which he sprang, the rock on which he built. As a noumenon—as an entity—Shelley stands alone; as a phenomenon in the stream of history he occupies the supreme place in the development of the thought and literature of eighteenth century England. In him the rational and the irrational, the imaginative and the intellectual meet; in him, as in no other man except Goethe, the currents of thought and feeling which had welled up through two hundred years of European civilization fuse into unity.

Shelley and his Contemporaries

> "The world's great age begins anew,
> The golden years return. . . ."

In such words did Shelley, in the final chorus of "Hellas," hail the dawn of a new world to come—that ideal world of perfect freedom and perfect love in which he so passionately believed. His eyes would have opened wide to hear the judgment of posterity that that very period in which he lived—the mad, unquiet day of war and turmoil—was itself perhaps the nearest approach which man has ever made to his envisioned Golden Age. It was the time of great misery and wrong, of the retreat from Moscow and the oppression of Greece and the Peterloo Massacre; tyrants and priests still pulled their age-old strings; the world still raised its topless pyramid of blood and gold; men still killed and men still died. And Custom, as Custom has a way of doing, remained and loosened its stifling, petrifying grip not one whit. The world of hours and days, of living men and their deeds, changes but little from generation to generation and from age to age; goodness and wisdom continue, evil and ignorance continue, and the society of twentieth century New York is fundamentally no better and no worse than the society of Nineveh and Tyre. A practical utopia was no nearer at hand in Georgian England than at any other given time in the history of civilization. Men may well be weary of the past, but to break with it is another matter—a matter that only a madman such as Shelley would proclaim and demand. It is superfluous to add that the erring world did not oblige him. Post-Revolution Europe retained its feet of clay.

But its spirit was truly golden; for from this warring and turbulent time, which communally was so significantly imperfect, there arose individual thinkers and singers of enormous stature whose legacy to the future, fostered and brought into being by the times, purified and idealized by their individual spirits, is richer than that of any other age. The contemporary world, subjective in its judgment, demands practical results; posterity, from the safe vantage ground of objectivity, does honor to intentions and to spirit. It makes little difference in the ultimate scales whether or not the Holy Grail is found, whether or not the Crusades are successful, whether or not the French Revolution is a practical success or a practical failure. What does matter is the impelling, unquenchable spirit of Galahad and Cœur-de-Lion and the great galaxy of aspiring men who dreamed and built a hundred years ago. The imperfect world of fact was the very soil in which their perfect world of vision took root; it was the suffering, diseased body which housed the infinite soul. Without bigotry there can be no Voltaire; without ignorance there can be no Kant; without drabness there can be no Beethoven; without weakness there can be no Napoleon; without chaos there can be no Goethe; and without evil there can be no Shelley. Beauty springs from ugliness, and revolution from oppression. The glory of the last Golden Age is not that it "accomplished" something in the vulgar sense of the word but that in a world of wrong and misery and ignorance and pitiful half-measures its greatest voices cried out that these things should not be so. Human society bumps along upon its dubious way; war and corruption and meanness continue as placidly as though five thousand years had not decried them and deplored them and signed protocols against them. But the mind and the spirit of individual man is wider, deeper, and more free for the lives and the works of the great liberators of the era of the French Revolution.

The intellectual tradition which Shelley inherited was, as has been pointed out, the creation of men who were profoundly conscious of their missions as liberators. The earlier men were for the most part simply iconoclasts, and Voltaire had sounded their war-cry once and for all in his famous "Ecrasez L'Infame!" It was not until the old order had been pulled down that men were at liberty to build for themselves; it was a long and slow procession to the heights, and throughout there was a vast variety of method and point of view. But the one bond remained, and, in retrospect upon the age as a whole, it was indissoluble: the striving for freedom, for emancipation. The octogenarian Goethe, looking back upon his full, rich life of activity and creation, evaluated himself thus: "If I were to say what I had really been to the Germans in general, and to the young German poets in particular, I should say I had been their liberator." Heine, whose life lapped over into a later age, but who in spirit was a true child of the Revolution, said of himself: "I trouble myself very little whether people praise my verses or blame them. But lay upon my coffin a sword; for I was a soldier in the warfare for the liberation of humanity." And Shelley himself, in his preface to "Prometheus Unbound": "Let this opportunity be conceded to me of acknowledging that I have what a Scotch philosopher characteristically terms a 'passion for reforming the world'." Or, more typically, in the high, singing invocation of the "Ode to the West Wind":

> "Drive my dead thoughts over the universe
> Like withered leaves to quicken a new birth!
> . . . .
> Be through my lips to unawakened earth
> The trumpet of a prophecy."

Could three poets be imagined more utterly dissimilar than these? Goethe, placid, Olympian, great with experience and understanding; Heine, jeering, suffering, wholly unintegrated, who never knew a calm moment in his life; Shelley, the madman, who could scarcely see the earth for his absorption in the heavens. Yet in each of them, however different their methods and their personalities, we find the underlying devotion to the spirit of freedom which the age of the great revolution planted in its sons.

In the earlier days of the satirists, philosophers, and pamphleteers the revolt had been for the most part against social and political tradition. This championship of liberty in its more practical aspects by no means died out —witness the bitter assaults of Heine on Philistinism

PHENOMENON

and the indignant fury of Shelley himself on the occasion of the disgraceful butchery at Manchester—but the tendency was ever away from the world of men and things towards the realm of ideas. Philosophy developed through Berkeley, Locke and Hume, and reached its apogee in the metaphysics of Immanuel Kant; in the Germanic countries music flew suddenly free of its century-old bondage to rule and form, and touched the heights; poetry ceased to be a simple matter of phrasing clever thoughts in pleasing metres and made the universe its province. Of all the forms of human expression the fine arts alone went their ordered, uneventful way; they had had their day three hundred years before. In every other sphere there was amazing activity. As if by a preconcerted signal in the last decades of the eighteenth century the spirit of creative man welled up within him and indulged in the most splendid of its sprees. No other age has produced its equal, not even time-hallowed Periclean Greece nor the more diffuse upheaval of the Renaissance. Consider the names: Goethe, Beethoven, Kant, Napoleon, Byron, Wordsworth, Schiller, Hegel, Keats, Shelley. Added to these greatest a host of minor men, of movements and counter-movements. Where was the old social-minded rationalism to be found in this galaxy of imaginative genius? For the most part it was gone. Imagination had at last touched the solid, earthly stuff of thought and transmuted it into song. The collectivism, the humanitarianism of the old days remained as a firm intellectual groundwork for the greatest minds; but in its highest manifestations the spirit of the time had changed, or better, had developed into something so much loftier than its original self as to appear altogether different. The watchword of Freedom remained. But prose had become poetry, reason had become imaginative understanding, truth had become beauty, thought had become song. Men raised their eyes from earth and stretched their fingers at the universal sun. It was the bright noonday of Faust and Prometheus and Napoleon. It was the perfect ripening of individualism.

Among his contemporaries in England Shelley stood alone. He was a truer child of his age than anyone except the inevitable Goethe and the inevitable Napoleon, and like them his position is at the pinnacle of a long development. The other great romantic poets fit less perfectly into the scheme of the times; they were not, like Shelley, comprehensive in their interests or fundamentally expressive of their age in its totality. They were poets—great poets—and each of them, according to his lights, was a true representative of his time; they are not, however, as tremendously significant historically as he was. Shelley was a symbol and a force; they were not. They lack his universality and inevitability. Wordsworth, Coleridge and Keats were the supreme "poets of escape." The first two, in their youth, had hailed the coming of the Revolution with joy and anticipation; they too had dreamed bright, gaudy dreams of happy Erewhons and had planned their promised land on the banks of the euphonious Susquehanna. But the brutal reality of bloody gutters and the whining guillotine and the carnage of Napoleon proved too much for them. Wordsworth took up celandines, Coleridge opium, and between them they created poetry of surpassing beauty. Their descent is not from the main stream of eighteenth century rationalism, as was Shelley's, but from the early romantic poets of that unromantic age—from Thomson and Gray and Cowper and Blake and Burns, sensitive spirits who had fled the con-

PHENOMENON

fusion of men and deeds and noisy unrest and sought in nature the peace and inspiration which they could not find elsewhere. "The world is too much with us," declared Wordsworth, and forthwith he turned his back upon that world. In doing so he enabled himself to become the incomparable poet of nature and the simple life; but at the same time he shut out behind him, as with an impenetrable wall, the vast, chaotic world of immediate reality which hurt him and which he could not understand.

Keats, though endowed with a richer imagination and a deeper emotional nature than Wordsworth, fundamentally looked at the world from the same point of view. At no time did he exhibit an interest in the march of events which was shaking Europe to its foundations; in him there is no trace whatsoever of the great humanistic tradition which was the rockbed of Shelley's flights. He was artist first, last, and all the time, and as an artist—dealing imaginatively with sensuous impressions—he was perhaps the greatest in English history. But, as was the case with Wordsworth and Coleridge, his glory was also his limitation; in his quest for ideal beauty he lost contact with the rough and ugly but, withal, aspiring and strangely gorgeous stuff of human life. No one can rob these three men of their greatness as poets. They were more truly romantic than Shelley, who at bottom was not a romantic at all, in that they lived not for ideas but for images and looked at things not in the hope of drawing some thought therefrom but for the sake of the thing itself. Judged by the standards of today, in which romantic poetry is adjudged the best poetry and the love of "the thing" for its own sake is held up as the most worthy artistic creed, Wordsworth and Keats (perhaps even Coleridge) are the equals—some say the superiors—

of Shelley as poets. As poets, yes. As artists in words and as builders of images they have never been surpassed. But they were *only* poets, and Shelley was more. Their world was beautiful, but it was a world of escape; they were much like our modern aesthetic school in that they relied too entirely upon the senses. Whereas the preceding age had undervalued the imagination, they undervalued the intellect. They were artists, well-nigh perfect artists. But they did not see life whole. They did not think.

Byron, on the other hand, thought too much. And thinking, as Goethe pointed out, was bad for him. The impulse was there, but the ability was not, and the result was that he fell apart into a multiple personality, each part of him at war with the other. He was not a romantic, like Wordsworth and Keats, nor an intellect aflame, like Shelley; he was simply a battleground on which all attitudes met and conflicted, and no victor ever appeared to take the field. He went in all directions at once and in no one direction for more than five minutes at a time. He felt deeply, but not constantly; he had to think, and his thought was muddled. Looking out upon the world through the ever-changing lens of his moods, he could find in it no values to which he might cling and in which he might wholeheartedly believe, and looking inward at himself he could discover no true self at all. Byron was cursed with the same "Zwiespältigkeit," or duality of nature, as Heinrich Heine. He was built on a nobler scale than his German contemporary, but his greatness and his misery sprang from the same source. Both are typical, if unhappily exaggerated, examples of that disintegration of personality which was to wreak so much unhappiness among the thinkers and poets of the age immediately following the outburst of "the Liberators." They were deficient in love, for they did not know what was worth loving and what was not; they were deficient in wisdom, for they did not know what was true and what was false. The result was a sardonic smile and a bleeding heart. The vivid color of Byron hid his basic weakness from his contemporaries; the splendor of his gestures atoned for their emptiness. Even Goethe was misled by the glamor of the man to attribute to him an apocalyptic sublimity which he did not possess and to apotheosize him in the figure of Euphorion, child of Faust and Helen. He mistook frenzy for passion, fury for strength, and "Weltschmerz" for imaginative understanding. He gave to Byron the place that in truth belonged to Shelley.

It has been necessary to treat at some length of Byron's strange and compelling personality in order that we may find his fundamental relationship to Shelley. He does not fit so comfortably into a niche as do Wordsworth and Keats; he was neither a pure poet of the senses nor yet an intellect. Raised in much the same tradition as Shelley, he did not have the centripetal, unifying force to assimilate what he thought and felt. He was deeply influenced by the baroque-romantic school; the soul-torn, brooding superman-de-luxe of a hundred Gothic novels reached his heyday in the "Byronic hero." And running side by side with the flamboyant stream there was the opposed current of the old rationalism, which, however, he could never muster into a semblance of order. His inheritance was the same as Shelley's, and he was possessed, moreover, of the supreme poetic yearning for universality; what he lacked was unity and strength. Don Juan is a shattered Prometheus. Like the great Titan he felt within him a blind, mad ecstasy of desire, but for what—toward what—he did not know. He had no Demogorgon to point him out the way. Byron aspired greatly, but his spirit cracked and shivered into splinters upon those rocks through which Shelley drove like a whirlwind. The one stood upon the pinnacle of a long development; consecrated to "the Idea" of which he and his poetry were the supreme expression, he was afire with an accumulated driving-power that was irresistible. The other strove for the pinnacle, floundered from one path onto another, and fell into an abyss. Byron was too human to be what he tried to be. He was diffuse where Shelley was concentrated, weak where Shelley was strong. Strange as it may sound, he was sane where Shelley was mad.

And now again we revert to those two of Shelley's contemporaries who alone with him stand out as the perfect symbols of the age in which they lived: Goethe and Napoleon. How dissimilar these three men were in their inner and outer lives, and yet, how alike in their final significance! Their differences are too ridiculously obvious to mention; their affinities lie deeper and concern them rather as symbols than as men. The Corsican and the German have reaped greater glory from posterity because in the large sense they were greater men. Buonaparte was as mad as Shelley—he was equally a straight line in a world of curves and angles—but his province was the earth; he turned the force that was in him into overt acts. And Goethe was as enamoured of the spirit of man as Shelley; but, while retaining his terrific intensity, he was still able to attain to a comprehensiveness of interest and experience which the other wholly lacked. But this is not the place to attempt evaluations. Whatever their individual excellencies and limitations may be, these three giants are alike in that they stand together at the pinnacle of the third Golden Age, and in themselves epitomize the spirit which, arising in the rational humanitarianism of the eighteenth century and developing through the portentous years of the French Revolution, found in their lives and works its supreme expression. They were all liberators, and they were all affirmers of the glory and significance of the *individual*. Therein lies their bond and their common significance in the history of civilization. Napoleon, uprooting empires and modelling the face of Europe to his desires; Goethe, aloof from the stress and strain of passing events and encompassing in his mighty spirit almost every field of human endeavor; Shelley, all spirit, all idea, headed all in one direction: the three of them were alike in this, that they were the logical culminating points of that slow, magnificent march of civilization whose end was the supremacy of the ideal over the real, of the individual over the group, of Man over men. To make use of Goethe's phrase, they taught the world "to live from within outward"; they set the standard of living and thinking, once for all, inside every man instead of outside him; they were living proofs that man's life and work, his mind and spirit, his "Doing" and "Being" should be—and can be—one. It is cheering in these mechanistic days of behaviorism, heredity and environment to look back upon their bright, golden time of rampant individualism: upon Faust and Prometheus, upon Goethe, Shelley and Napoleon. For they are the greatest men of an age of great men; they are the supreme examples, each in his own way, of what human personality at its most powerful and most free may be; they remain to remind us of a later day who live in the shadow of forces which we have bent to our will but which we do not understand, that the one real and enduring glory of the world is the free, aspiring spirit of man. And perhaps, by their lives more than by their works, by what they eternally *are* more than by what they once *did*, they can still, in the words of Goethe, teach us

> "Uns von Halben zu entwöhnen
> Und im Ganzen, Guten, Schönen
> Resolut zu leben."

Shelley and his Successors

The world has changed a great deal in the last hundred years. This is at one and the same time an edgeless platitude and a magic shibboleth to many sesames; for not only may it be directed toward such impressively obvious facts as the impeachment of meadows by alleyways, of clipper ships by quadruple-screw turbined liners, of flintlocks by howitzers, and of God by "natural selection," but also, in a slightly subtler way, toward many of those deeper and loftier by-products of civilization which we have grown to believe—since we wish so to believe—are as ageless and immutable as man from whom they generate. Such a by-product is poetry, revered and cherished through the centuries as something a wee bit above and beyond the material and cultural changes which the uprolling years may bring; and even the most determinedly hard-headed of us is loath to admit that that which we feel to be so close and essential to the human spirit is subject, even as are waistcoats and national frontiers and the morals of young ladies, to the flux of days and years. Poetry, we would believe, however much it may be tempered and refined in the crucible of art to conform to the tastes of this or that artist or era, is in its basic nature an instinctive, spontaneous thing. Men breathe, we say, men eat and sleep and hope and fear and sing and write great verse with a fine indifference as to

PHENOMENON

whether the material earth be at that particular moment in the possession of Alexander or Napoleon or the bespectacled physicist in the nearest laboratory. But is this so?

Assuredly singers have sung and poets have made verse in every age from the Beginning to the Now; but though the form and the name of their art has remained unchanged, surely the highest and lowest of what we call poetry are so different as to seem of entirely discrete origin and purpose. Poetry, since we must use the term to cover all, is indeed a constant; but the quality of poetry—the ultimate, intrinsic beauty and wisdom and truth of it as the expression of living men—changes ever with the life and the world from which it springs. Men sing best in the early morning: at midday they see too well and are too busy; in the afternoon they are too refined, too worldly; in the evening they are too tired. Men sang in the bright, high-promising mornings of the ages of Pericles and of the High Renaissance; they sang best of all in the age of the French Revolution. Shelley and Goethe and Beethoven, the three supreme artistic spirits of the last Golden Age, lived and created in an old, well founded world into which there had just blown the breath of a wild high-hearted surmise of things to come—a world blessed at one and the same time by solid realities and heaven-scaling idealities, by the sanity and by the promise of morning. Eyes were ahead; they were at the threshold of the day, and they sang because there was a song in their hearts.

> "Bliss was it in that dawn to be alive,
> But to be young was very heaven."

It is a perhaps lamentable but undeniably definite fact that neither dawn nor youth are made of stuff that long endures, and that splendid moment of vigor and vision which Wordsworth hailed was no exception. Hard upon its heels there came a crash.

The first shock of the débâcle was too much for the tenderer spirits. Wordsworth, Coleridge and Keats in England, the whole Romantic School in Germany, turned with loathing or indifference from the French Revolution, whose coming they had welcomed as an ideality but whose brutal, factual reality was more than they could bear. The tougher spirits, the men of wide comprehension who were the truest children of their age, were more jealous of their vision. They tolerated the ugly actuality for the beauty of "the Idea" which was still alive and flaming; they recognized that that hoarse cry of "Liberté!" which arose from the red cobblestones of the Place de la Concord was in essence the same as that pure and infinitely more lofty cry of Liberty to which they were consecrating their lives. Beethoven listened to the guns of Europe and sang of pain and triumph in pain; Goethe saw in Buonaparte an individual and a symbol whose very existence was alone worth the confusion and misery of thirty years; Shelley, maddest prophet of them all, affirmed to the end, believing that the carnage of a hundred battlefields was but the earthly manifestation—deplorable in itself yet glorious in the greater scheme—of a liberation of the spirit which was to come. The supreme figures of the age, the liberators, the affirmers, were secure upon their pinnacles. They sang the last great swan-song of a dying order, and when they fell in death, the era which in them had reached its culmination fell too. For vaster, stranger things than mere political revolutions were at hand.

In time to come, when the God of Science has made either divinities or mechanisms out of its worshippers, men will be able to see more clearly the outlines and development of that new chapter of human history which began in the early decades of the nineteenth century and has unfolded with steady acceleration up to the present day. Then they will realize that the great upheaval, which in the brief span of a century has worked such undreamed changes in the material earth and in the scope of man's power and knowledge, has to an equal degree left its mark upon the deeper, subtler machinery of his spirit. We have said that the supreme men of the Revolutionary Age looked forward. The "claims of the ideal" were strong upon them; they aspired and sang. Today, as for the past century, the eyes of the greatest are no longer ahead, and the vista of an ideal future has been supplanted by the blurred immensity of a very real present. Science and democracy and that whole tangled infinity of newborn knowledge and power and value which we call "modern civilization" have descended upon us, and that day, which from the threshold of a century ago could still be hailed as one of surpassing beauty and spiritual liberty, is now so much about us and upon us that we cannot see its direction, for its chaos, nor its meaning, for its incomprehensibility. We are too busy building to judge, too busy learning to understand; a world of *things* has poured itself upon us and we must adjust ourselves to it. When with time the mess has become a little clearer and we stand at last upon that fine, high eminence from which we may simultaneously look back, with understanding, at the structure we have raised, and forward, with vision, at the untrodden uplands that lie still ahead, then again will there be a Golden Age of Song. Meanwhile we write great prose, and think great thoughts, and ask many questions.

In the modern world (and by the modern world we

mean that new order which arose a century ago and continues still) poetry is not—and cannot be—the vehicle of expression for the greatest minds and spirits. Democracy, communism, industrialism, selective evolution, world wars, and the quantum theory—all those unnumbered things and concepts which, like the iron warriors of Jason, have risen overnight from the age-old, reliable greenness of the earth—cannot yet be expressed supremely in song. First they must be conquered and wrought into meaningful being; first the spirit of man must catch up with his mind and his hands. It is an age of thinkers, not of singers. The poets of the new order cannot express the soul and meaning of their world, as could Shelley and Goethe theirs a hundred years ago. They can no longer rise to that inner all-embracing comprehension of the significance of things which is the beginning and the end of the greatest poetic genius. The "Weltgeist" is no longer possible. The poet's field is limited, and the idea of limited poetry is in itself almost a contradiction. How can we expect nineteenth and twentieth century verse to be truly great, when the new, strange world in which life finds itself moving is as yet unopened to it? Or how can we expect it to hold a supreme position in the regard and affections of men, when those things in which men are primarily engrossed are precisely those it may not touch? Poetry is no longer the most true and most comprehensive expression of the spirit of man. It has lost its all-combining universality. It has lost its fundamental unity with life.

Poetry on the grand scale being no longer possible, writers of verse in the last century have branched off into two fairly well-defined byways: the poetry of the material world and the poetry of escape. Wordsworth, Coleridge and Keats, as has been pointed out, concerned themselves little, if at all, with the world of men and events; they built upon the tradition of the earlier nature poets and in them romantic poetry, the poetry of escape, came to its final and perhaps finest fruition. One usually thinks of these men as more conservative, less modern than Shelley; but, whereas he was a coping-stone of the old order, they were the foundations of the new. Of the lesser poets of the time, Landor, Hood, and Tom Moore were fundamentally romantic in spirit. Southey, as was to be expected of a poet-laureate, was a hangover from the eighteenth century. The rise of romanticism was amazing, both in its suddenness and in its widespread influence. In Germany Brentano and Arnim sounded the call with a collection of folk and nature poetry, "Der Knaben Wunderhorn," in the same year that Wordsworth and Coleridge published the "Lyrical Ballads"; and close upon their heels came the romantic schools of Tieck, Novalis, Uhland, Rückert, Eichendorff, Chamisso, and a host of other men who sought refuge in nature, medievalism, the Orient, and indeed anything in which they might find the beauty that was nowhere perceptible in the world of their own day. It is typical of the German national character that three "philosophers of escape" should also arise: Fichte, Schelling and Friedrich Schlegel, with one "romantic theologian," Schleiermacher, in the bargain. In France aestheticism took root in the verse of Gautier, de Vigny, de Musset and their "Parnassian" brotherhood of pearls and tears. And in England, always less addicted than its sister-countries to formal "schools" and "movements," the romantic tradition waxed and expanded in the works of individuals down through the whole length of the Victorian Age. Tennyson's tremendous popularity in his own time is largely owing to the fact that he was the poet of escape, par excellence, in an age which in its deeper nature was primarily one of escape also. In the face of the industrial revolution and the birth of science, the social world of England stiffened and contracted, buried its head in the comfortable sands of convention and "good sense" rather than bear the burden of the storm that had broken. In poetry men looked for a sedative rather than a stimulus, for peace rather than strife and a call to arms. Tennyson supplied their needs with consummate art. Arnold and Swinburne, greater spirits though lesser artists than the Laureate, yearned for a universality to which, being created in the fabric and pattern of their time, they could not attain. The former sallied out upon the world in his early youth, found it to be only a darkling plain of confusion and frustration, and relapsed into a wan and melancholy acquiescence. The latter, with a truer instinct for free, passionate song than any man since Shelley, dreamed of an ideal freedom which he could find nowhere on the jumbled, ambiguous earth and became the poet of the older, clearer, cleaner days of classical antiquity. Shelley had affirmed; Swinburne negated. The child of the Revolution had sung of victory and life; the Victorian sang of rest and peace and dreamless death. Perhaps no better comparison of the spirit of poetry in the two eras is furnished than that of the closing stanza of "The Skylark":

> "Teach me half the gladness
> That thy brain must know,
> Such harmonious madness
> From my lips would flow
> The world should listen then—
> as I am listening now."

and these lines from "The Garden of Proserpine":

PHENOMENON

> "I am weary of days and hours,
> Blown buds and barren flowers,
> Desires and dreams and powers
> And everything but sleep."

The romantic tradition of later days has not lacked great artists: Morris, the Rossettis, Stevenson, Francis Thompson, Yeats, De la Mare—the list is long and illustrious. They are all great artists, great makers of beautiful images, and sensitive interpreters of various moods and soul-states. But their field is limited, for they are poets of escape. They dare not *think*, for in their world thought and beauty are incompatible. No better example of the existing state of affairs can be found than William Morris, who combined within himself the twin personalities of a social thinker and a medievalist and who kept these two in separate, hermetically sealed compartments of his nature between which no contact was possible. His poetry was his escape. And for the others, though less obviously, it is the same. The men of aspiring spirit—the Arnolds and Swinburnes—who have made an effort at comprehensive understanding and have found only frustration, are singers in the minor key. The others admit candidly, however unconsciously, that this vast crazy-quilt of loud-speakers and zeppelins and shower-baths-in-every-room and glandular secretions and proposed rockets to Mars is scarcely as yet a safe and sane dwelling place for the shy Muses. Feeling within them the quenchless love of beauty but realizing simultaneously that that beauty is to be found nowhere in the hurly-burly world of things, these men have—each after his own desire—built themselves a world in which to live and from which to shape the fabrics of their verse. Here some one may point out that Shelley too, more perhaps than any other poet,

MAD SHELLEY

lost himself in his ideal world. He did. But his world, far from being one of escape, was one that was solidly founded upon that lower, deeper world of thought and reality. Not for an instant did he forget the cry of suffering and unredeemed mankind that echoed from below. Shelley was not Ariel—he was Prometheus. It is the later romantic poets who have tried to forget.

Romanticism has been the chief, but not the only, current of poetry which has arisen with the new order. About the middle of the nineteenth century a group of men arose in England and America who have sought to take the material world by the horns and mould it into the stuff of art. The first—perhaps the greatest—of these "robust poets" was Robert Browning; his tradition has been developed and expanded in the verse of Whitman, Henley, Masefield, Kipling and Carl Sandburg. These men, unlike the tenderer romantics, have taken the world of living fact as their raw material and have sought to travel from reality to ideality rather than in the opposite direction; but, like them, their province is limited. Seeking gallantly if futilely to give expression to a newborn world, they have in their treatment of what they believe to be realities invariably been forced to sacrifice form to fidelity and concept to actuality; they have, each in his own way, sought to face the facts, and each, though an able poet, has in the larger sense failed. They can describe things perfectly, affirming, rejoicing in their very being, but they cannot understand them, and without understanding all poetry can be only a shadow of its true self. The greatest of these yea-sayers, Browning and Whitman, have been called "barbarians" by Santayana. They are animal in their high spirits, blind in their affirmation; their militant virility is at once their glory and their

PHENOMENON

limitation. Stronger than the romantics, their poetry is no wiser, and less beautiful. If the verse of Tennyson is emasculated, that of Browning is despiritualized. Setting their cap for reality, the "robust poets" have been able to see the world and, in a measure, to feel it; but they have not understood it imaginatively. In the last analysis, they are superficial.

It is more difficult to fit the sprawling immensity of the last century into the comfortable, ready-to-wear jacket of form and theory than it is with some of the earlier, more homogeneous ages of the past. Its direction, judged from its manifestations in the mental and spiritual life of men, seems to be from concentration toward diffuseness, from unity toward disintegration. This, it will be observed, is precisely the opposite of its manifestations in the material world. Beginning in the early decades of the eighteen-hundreds, when the first chimney of the first factory reared its prophetic ugliness up into Shelley's "bare blue pavilion of heaven," an incredible chaos of new things, new concepts, and new powers has been revealed to men. In a brief span of years the horizons of factual knowledge have expanded well-nigh limitlessly, and, armed with the weapons of a new science and a new social theory, we have in effect created another world and another civilization upon the outworn ruins of the old. But our wisdom did not—and indeed cannot—keep pace with our knowledge; our spirits are as yet unable to comprehend what our hands and brains have wrought. The first shock was the hardest. With sickening suddenness men awoke to the fact that the world had changed overnight, that nature and God and the immemorially prescribed order of things were turning from their everlasting courses, that the good old days—the days of rationality and coherence, the days that had been since a certain progressive Pithecanthropus had swung from his tree into man's estate—were gone forever. A dazzling and inscrutable universe had opened to man; he had tools wherewith to work it, but he had no values by which he might weigh and measure it.

The result was what might be expected. Those loftier, more audacious spirits who would encompass all and who sought blindly for that universal understanding which was no longer to be found, suffered the most. Byron and Heine, those two significant precursors of the disintegrated modern man, asked more questions than the heavenly Aristophanes had any intention of answering, and alternately cried for the moon and jeered at themselves for doing so. Philosophy, which had seemed to have reached its "ultima thule" in the magnificent metaphysical structure of Kant, found the age-old foundations upon which it rested vanished suddenly from beneath its feet and staggered through the dog-days of Schopenhauer's pessimism and Nietzsche's hysterical self-assertiveness. Romantic poetry continued on its beautiful but cloistered way with an occasional detour into the decadence of Verlaine, Beaudelaire and Wilde, or the self-consciousness of the Imagists; the tradition of virile superficiality has not died out either and in recent years has swelled out in the easy formlessness of free verse. Of poetry on the grand scale there is none. The nearest approaches in the nineteenth century to a figure of heroic proportions in the once identical, now discrete, fields of thought and art are Victor Hugo, Richard Wagner and Leo Tolstoi, but to each of them there was denied that final imaginative understanding which they sought. Hugo lacked in depth what he possessed in breadth; Wagner, facing the universe and finding it wanting, was a pessimist, and his song, however noble, is ever in the minor key; and Tolstoi, earnest and uncompromising almost to the point of madness, had in the end to flee, without answers to his questions, to the embracing nepenthe of the orthodox church. The modern world wreaks its havoc upon those who would understand it whole.

Ours is an age of thought—in literature an age of prose. Poets, as Shelley would have them and, indeed, as in his day the greatest of them were, are no longer "the hierophants of an unapprehended inspiration; the mirrors of the gigantic shadows which futurity casts upon the present." They are no longer the unacknowledged legislators of the world. Modern civilization is in the hands of thinkers: Darwin, Spencer, Huxley, Pasteur, Claude Bernard, Einstein, Edison—it is they who are "the words which express what they understand not; the trumpets which sing to battle, and feel not what they inspire; the influence which is moved not, but moves;" it is they who are the true children of an age in which there is precious little to sing about but more than plenty to think about. They are the great specialists in an age of specialization, the great realists in an age of pressing realities. And in literature the field belongs to the novelist—the "artistic scientist," we may call him—for his eyes are bent toward earth and toward the earthly problems and relationships of our day. It is a significant fact that Germany, the most uncompromisingly idealistic of nations and the most indefatigable of bloodhounds on the trail of ever-elusive truth, has since 1850 produced the greatest novelists of the time and not one poet above the third rank. There is no mysticism in this; the best minds are simply the expression of the age itself. They move within its greater current. They seek that goal which it has set them. And today that goal is knowledge.

The modern world is wide and diffuse; we know much and are on the way to knowing more. Progress is made by specialization, by trained, despiritualized minds who pay close attention to the almighty *fact* and do not ask too many foolish questions. The universal intellect is today as impossible as the universal spirit; the von Humboldts are gone as well as the Goethes and Shelleys. The scientist in his laboratory may well be a master-unit in the march of progress, but as an individual his sphere is limited, even as is that of the poet. It is not the day for comprehensive spirits, for that highest imaginative understanding which fuses all things—the earth below and the heavens above and the soul within—into the supreme unity of song. For that we must wait until a greater measure of order has been wrought from the confused and overstuffed world in which we live. Meanwhile the thinker continues thinking and the poet continues feeling, each in his limited sphere, each according to his lights, and each building toward the day when again they may meet and become one. And meanwhile those unfortunates among us who cannot become very enthusiastic over even the most magnificent differential equation and for whom even the most perfectly turned of Amy Lowellesque images leaves something to be desired are at least vouchsafed the inspiration of looking back upon those universal spirits of a century ago—upon Goethe and Shelley and Buonaparte—to whom, more than to any other men, it was granted to be whole and complete expressions of the age in which they lived.

PHENOMENON

Shelley's Significance

Great men, no less than little men, are living, human organisms. They are born, they receive impressions for an allotted number of years, they react to those impressions for an allotted number of years, they die. Out of nothing they come willy-nilly into a world which they had no part in building, live for a while in that world, and pass from it, again willy-nilly, back into nothing. First and last they are individuals, they are entities. It remains for biographers and critics and presumptuous young gentlemen in the English departments of our universities to assign them their proper places in the larger scheme of things, to point out their significance in this or that movement or development, of which they themselves might well have been quite unconscious, to show why they were what they were and not otherwise. In considering Shelley it is imperative to keep this fact in mind; for he was, as we have been at some pains to emphasize, as much an entity, complete in himself, as any man who has ever lived. We shall attempt to treat him as such—as a noumenon—in the second part. In this first part we have treated him as a phenomenon, and in seeking to determine his relationships to his precursors, his contemporaries, and his successors we have, *propter quod*, launched fairly out into the realm of dogmatic theory. Dogmatic theories are notoriously dangerous things; and it is with the willing admission that historical interpretation is invariably colored by the interpreter's desire to build coherence out of chaos and to find order where perhaps none really exists that we present Shelley in the rôle of a landmark and a symbol in the stream of civilization.

Of precisely what have we found him to be the symbol? Just what is his position in his age and the position of that age in the flux of ages? We have called the period in which he lived a *golden* one, and, from the quantity and the stature of its great figures, it seems to merit the title. Shelley himself was aware that he moved in a world of great thought and great song, witness his statement in "A Defense of Poetry": "In spite of the low-thoughted envy which would undervalue contemporary merit, our own will be a memorable age in intellectual achievements, and we live among such philosophers and poets as surpass beyond comparison any who have appeared since the last national struggle for civil and religious liberty." He saw it was an age of great men, of liberators, and he saw too that it was not by blind chance that they were grouped together in the space of a few generations. With an amazing perspicacity he realized the fundamental, the ultimate significance of the era of the French Revolution of which he himself was so perfect an expression. "Mankind appears to me to be emerging from their trance. I am aware methinks of a slow, gradual, silent change." And again, he writes: "It is impossible to read the compositions of the most celebrated writers of the present day without being startled with the electric life that burns in their words. They measure the circumference and sound the depths of human nature with a comprehensive and all-penetrating spirit, and they are themselves perhaps the most astonished at its manifestations; *for it is less their spirit than the spirit of the age.*"

The spirit of the age. Freedom—complete and universal Individualism. And the three giants through whom it spoke most nobly were Goethe, Napoleon, and Shelley. The German, broad as he was intense, deep as he was lofty, human as he was divine, embraced in the tremendous scope of his personality all the experiences of man and lived the

PHENOMENON

fullest and most perfectly comprehensive life that has been lived on earth. He was the greatest of the three. The Corsican was all personality, all "self," and by the very marvel of the indomitable will which flamed within him he remains, for better or worse, the compelling symbol of the most rampant individualism which the world has seen. He was the strongest of the three. The Englishman, in the last analysis the strangest of them all, lived to be not quite thirty. All but unknown in his day, he is still, a century later, less known than the other two of the great triumvirate. And he will remain less known, because he lacked the spiritual breadth of appeal of the one and the worldly strength of appeal of the other. He was all ideal, all song, all vision. And he was the most beautiful of the three.

The most beautiful, and something else besides. Let us let our eye rove for one moment back along that long and splendid ascent from the earthly rationalism of the eighteenth century to the pinnacle upon which he stood; let it look again upon the débâcle which shook the civilized world in the early decades of the last century, when Bellerophon fell in shattered chaos; and finally let it come to rest upon Bellerophon himself, he who of all men had ridden Pegasus nearest to the sky. We see a spirit—a pure, flaming spirit—who, standing at the very culmination of an old age, was simultaneously in a position to look forward with joy to the coming of a new age whose dawn was breaking. The confusion of reality had not descended to mar the splendor of the ideal. Firm on his foundation of intellect, aflame with the glory of vision, Percy Shelley threw back his head, in the face of the ugliness and ignorance and misery of earth, and sang his song of affirmation. . . . A beautiful song. A beautiful singer. It is not until we pause to consider how utterly alone he stood upon the crest of the third Golden Age, how much higher and more insistent than those of other singers was the sustained note that he struck, and how perfectly he epitomizes that triplicate frenzy of poet, prophet and lover of which Plato had spoken two thousand years before, that we perceive his uniqueness, his "difference." Then we are able to see that, as a phenomenon in the stream of history, he was less a part than a product of human society, less a man of his age than a child of his age, less a soldier in the army of great liberators than the song itself which that army sang. Then we recognize that, in his historical setting, he is less a human being than an emanation of the world-spirit, an ultimate, gorgeous gesture to mark the passing of an old world and the coming of a new, a refined and intensified incarnation of the universal song of man.

We see him thus. We see other men. Then suddenly, inevitably, we know that Shelley was mad.

PART II

NOUMENON

The Poet's Land
>"Wer den Dichter will verstehen
>Muss in Dichters Lande gehen."

THE words are Goethe's. It is good advice; it is hard advice. In the case of Shelley it is at one and the same time imperative and impossible to follow. For he, over and above all other men, lived in a world that was wholly and exclusively his own, and exhibited, both in the processes of his thought and feeling and in the conduct of his active life, a personality of which it may be said quite baldly, without fear of exaggeration or falsification, that there has been nothing like it in the world before or since. He was not simply "different" in the sense that every human individual is unlike all other human individuals; nor was he unique only in the sense that all genius is unique. Genius, as we have come to know it, manifests itself in infinite variety—else it would forfeit its name and being; but its very irregularity is in a measure regular, and its course, as it has exhibited itself here and there, now and again, in the history of mankind, has tended in certain fairly distinct directions, along fairly well defined lines. There have been intellectual geniuses, military geniuses, imaginative geniuses, scientific geniuses. Down through millennia great minds and spirits have arisen to match themselves against the numberless problems which have been set to men; they have hurled their strength against widely dissimilar horizons, they have followed different paths, used different tools, worked toward different ends. But, to borrow a phrase from the poet, there is similarity to be found in their difference, an underlying generic unity in their diversity. Admitting their individuality as patent, it is still possible to relate and correlate them one to another, to show that while A and B were unlike in attitude they were similar in craftsmanship, and while X and Y held opposed artistic creeds they concurred in intellectual matters; in short, to find a measure of likeness. Napoleon has his Alexander, Shakespeare his Sophocles, Milton his Dante, Einstein his Euclid, Kant his Plato. We call Wordsworth and Keats "romantic" poets and at once are able to name a score of men who, if below them in ability, are nevertheless like them in attitude and purpose. We mention Newton, and there comes to mind the long succession of illustrious scientific thinkers from Copernicus to Faraday. We conjure up Hippocrates, and presto! we have Pasteur. Homer suggests comparisons with the creators of "Beowulf" and the "Niebelungenlied"; Aristophanes with Byron and Heine, Caesar with Mussolini, Robespierre with Lenin, Edison with Archimedes, Mohammed with Genghis Khan. In almost every case there are to be found affinities between great men; unique as genius may be in its varied, individualized aspects, there have been but the smallest handful of men of whom it can truthfully be said that they resemble none other than themselves. Setting aside for the moment the great religious teachers, there are only three. Aristotle stands alone. So does Goethe. So does Shelley. No one—to filch a beautifully applicable line from Boswell—can be said to put you in mind of Shelley.

The Greek and the German stand apart from lesser

NOUMENON

great men largely by virtue of their stature and of their enormous comprehensiveness of outlook, from each other by their fundamental oppositeness of attitude. Shelley is not built upon their grand scale; his "difference" is not in size but in texture; he is fashioned not of a *greater* but of *another* fabric than normal men, and the keystone of his amazing personality is not, in the last analysis, that he thought more clearly or felt more deeply, or loved more beautifully than any one else, but that he was organized in a unique way. All people who knew him bare witness to his strange unlikeness not only to normal man but to normal genius; so did those of his contemporaries who knew him only through his notorious deeds; so do we of today who know him through the vicarious, depersonalized medium of his writings; he himself bore witness best of all. In his every action and every word he was a living anomaly, a perfect and irrefutable proof of his own "difference." The mainspring of his nature is not to be found in any one of those many facets which he has presented to the world—not in the magic of his fancy nor the wildness of his convictions nor in the insanity of his daily life—but in his united, integral *self*. The one, the only, all-important fact to be remembered when dealing with the man is that he was "put together" in another way and "worked" in another way than we; and it is precisely this fact which has so often been lost sight of, with the result that the genuine Shelley is being either sentimentalized or denounced into an "immortality of oblivion."

In general we are permitted one of two conceptions of the poet: either he was a sweet and sensitive Ariel, astray in a tough and inconsiderate world of men, or he was a mad, unstable young fool whom it was positively dangerous to leave at large; either he was the dear, pettable, if rather ridiculous, charm-monger that has appealed to Henry van Dyke and Elinor Wylie or he was the immoral young menace that emphatically did not appeal to Lord Elden and some goodly thousands of worthy Regency Britishers; either, in brief, he was a dreamer or a misfit—maybe both. Of course he was both. So was Jesus Christ. So is the open-collared sophomore across the hall who feels a mild urge toward wildflowers and Buddhism. So is the wretched syphilitic in the nearest lunatic asylum. Shelley was many things to many men; but he was neither a Messiah nor a crank nor a sufferer from a venereal disease. He can be seen in many lights, but it is a woful mistake to take one or another of his aspects at its face value without referring it to the whole of which it is so integral a part. For he was whole—more whole, indeed, more completely an organized personality, than any man who ever walked and suffered and sang upon the surface of the earth. He was a dreamer; he was a misfit. Well and good. "Hamlet" is a tragedy in five acts treating of a young man who could not make up his mind. There is as much profit in approaching Shelley, the noumenon, objectively as in approaching the Venus de Milo with a ruler and protractor. Treating him as a phenomenon, that method is all very well. For there we seek knowledge. Treating him as an entity, as a personality, it is not well at all. For here we seek not knowledge but imaginative understanding. And the first, indeed the only, step which we must take at the outset of this quest is to enter as best we may into the poet's land and then to look about us with the poet's eyes. Camels may not pass through the eyes of needles, nor may any one of us, who feels so inclined, force himself by some stereotyped formula of spiritual gymnastics abruptly into Shelley's untrodden domain. But we can try; and perhaps it will be by forgetting for a moment that we are awesomely sophisticated people in an awesomely complex world that we shall find most success. For Shelley's world was simple, and Shelley was a child.

The Child

> "Not in entire forgetfulness
> And not in utter nakedness,
> But trailing clouds of glory do we come
> From God, who is our home:
> Heaven lies about us in our infancy!"

On the fourth of August, 1792, Percy Bysshe Shelley was born at Field Place, in the parish of Warnham, Sussex. The eldest son of a well established family whose position was somewhere along the line which divides the upper squirarchy from the lower peerage, his early life was passed rationally enough and under auspices good enough to have produced at least a tolerably honest lawyer or a pleasant country squire. Doubtless he developed and reacted in strictly obedient conformity to the respected laws of embryology and infant psychology, and doubtless much that he was and was later to be is attributable to his heredity (though *there* is a task for the eugenicist) and to his early environment and associations; but it is pleasanter, and perhaps wiser, to believe that he came into the world and into manhood what he was—wide-eyed and naïve and aflame, wanting only experience as nutriment, carrying from the very womb and from the nothingness beyond the womb that oneness and integrity of spirit which was ever and only his. To no child are the "Intimations" of Wordsworth so applicable as to him. It is difficult to think of Timothy Shelley and Elizabeth Pilfold as completely his father and mother; they seem rather to bear much the same relation toward their child that Shelley later felt himself to bear toward his poetry. They were "the hierophants of an unapprehended inspiration," the mediums through which a spirit of which they had not the least surmise chose to work its will. Through their bodies a child passed into the earth "from God, who was his home"; through them there transpired a force from infinity into sentient, individualized being. This smacks of mysticism, and mysticism at its best is flabby and unsatisfying. Occasionally, however, it is also unavoidable. It requires no exhaustive scrutiny into old Sussex archives to discover that there was there more of mystery than of genetic logic about the blue-eyed and doubtless lustily squalling brat who came to Field Place one August afternoon, in 1792.

From the very first Shelley was precocious. At home he had a commendable—or deplorable (depending on the point of view)—tendency toward "cuteness and whimsicality": his little sisters loved him for it; his parents shook their heads and bundled him off to school as soon as possible. Already, when scarcely out of the cradle, he was "different"; no single person who met him after he had reached the ripe age of five years and established his first contact with the world was ever to doubt that fact. Through the years under the Reverend Edwards of Warnham and Dr. Greenlaw of Sion House Academy and Headmaster Keate of Eton he followed his own path, as unswervingly as he was to follow it in his later, stranger years, with a fine disregard of any and all who tried to make of him what he was not. At the age when most boys, happily enough, resemble nothing in the world so much as semi-articulate fox-terriers, he possessed a more solid and coordinated personality than the average man of five times his years. And that personality was no easy burden to bear. Incessantly jeered at, incessantly picked on and tormented, by his masters no less than by his fellows, he knew peace only when alone and when in the company of his sisters during the vacation times at home. Only Elizabeth, Mary and Hellen accepted him with unquestioning childish wisdom for what he was; only himself understood himself. He paid the price of the misfit and suffered as only a sensitive, lonely adolescent can suffer. Nor is it our place to rail in righteous wrath at Greenlaw and Keate and Bethell and the embryonic squires of Eton who made his life what it was. Had they not persecuted him, he would never have rebelled; had they not been normal human beings, Shelley would not have been Shelley.

No, his pre-Oxford days were not happy ones, nor—even in tolerant retrospect at young genius—can they be called successful ones. But as he grew and read and mused and suffered most terribly from the ridicule and baiting of his schoolmates, a world and a universe were gradually unfolding before his eyes—a world embittered and stained by the ugliness and the pain of which his persecution at Eton was but a miniature, but a world too, he perceived, wherein somewhere there was beauty and truth and goodness and significance. These he must find, these he must give to men. That was all. Beset with such blind and aching "Weltschmerz" as only a fifteen-year-old can know, he would wander apart and think strange thoughts and weep strange tears, while from behind him in the school building there came the cries of his tormentors, and oppressors, and in his heart he took the sacred vow to which in all the years to come he was never once untrue:

MAD SHELLEY

> "I will be wise,
> And just, and free, and mild, if in me lies
> Such power, for I grow weary to behold
> The selfish, and the strong still tyrannize
> Without reproach or check."

"I then," he writes, "controlled my tears, my heart grew calm, and I was meek and bold." Neither meekness nor boldness ever forsook him. The uprolling years served only to strengthen and consolidate that incredible constancy of spirit which he had brought with him into the world and to the unsullied maintenance of which he devoted his life. The child of fifteen grew into the child of thirty; age came, and with it experience and wisdom and artistic mastery, but the permeating, motivating spirit—that essence which was not a part of the man nor an attribute of the man, but the man himself—remained identically the same. It is a far cry from the chaotic bathos of "Zastrozzi" and "The Wandering Jew" (in the tremendous length of which Thomas Campbell discovered exactly two creditable lines) to the artistic miracle of "Prometheus Unbound"; but at bottom there is precious little difference between the child who walked alone about the grounds of Eton and swore his solemnly boyish oath of consecration and the somewhat older, somewhat wiser child who concluded the greatest poem in the English language with these words:

> "To suffer woes which Hope thinks infinite;
> To forgive wrongs darker than death or night;
> To defy Power which seems omnipotent;
> To love, and bear; to hope till Hope creates
> From its own wreck the thing it contemplates;
> Neither to change, nor falter, nor repent;
> This, like thy glory, Titan, is to be
> Good, great and joyous, beautiful and free;
> This is alone Life, Joy, Empire, and Victory."

NOUMENON

Shelley never did "change, nor falter, nor repent." He never stooped to half measures, never permitted the massed opinion of the world to bend his will to its will. He disregarded the "rules of the game," because within him, as in a holy chalice, he bore his own conviction as to how the game should be played. Those shades of the prison-house of which Wordsworth spoke did not close upon this growing boy; the "vision splendid" remained, and the common daylight of maturity never brought to him, as it did to other men and, indeed, to Wordsworth himself, its adjusting leaven of dreamless acquiescence. The biographer of Shelley is set many tasks, but at least he is spared the demarcation of "periods" and "phases." Shelley grew, but he did not change. He preserved through all his life that internal sanctity of soul which he had brought with him into the world; he would not and could not make those adjustments to life which are the accepted hall-marks of maturity; he saw with the eyes of a child. And if the cynic chooses to add, "a rather backward child," there will be no one to contradict him.

For few fond parents would care to admit that their admired offspring were capable of as much damnfoolishness as was Shelley. The worldly sense, the social touch, develops early in children; it does not take them long to learn that it is bad manners to ask too many questions, that a lie is now and again considerably more helpful than the truth, and that what one may confide freely to the gang down on the corner one may emphatically not confide to one's papa and mama. And these are things which Shelley never learned at all. He possessed to the ultimate degree the small boy's love of defiance of authority, but he wholly lacked that counterbalancing awe for authority which in the end always compels the normal young anarchist back into the fold. In the earlier days of his lifelong defiance of Custom, he admittedly took a more or less malicious joy simply in shocking its high priests in whatever manner he might. There was much of this attitude, for example, in his program of circulating his immortally infamous "Defense of Atheism." But this pleasure was short-lived: he outraged too many and was outraged too deeply in return for the thrill to last. He was no inhibited conformist on a sudden reactionary jag; he was a professional bolshevik who threw his bombs because within him there flamed the passionate conviction that they *should* be thrown. More truthfully than of any man who ever lived it can be said of Shelley that he never spoke a word that he believed was untrue nor performed an act which he believed not to be right. He lived according to his lights and he followed the gleam, whether it led over mountain peaks or through sewers, with a constancy that is almost incredible. Whatever was wretched in his life, as well as whatever was noble and magnificent, sprang from his complete moral integrity—from the unshakable belief in the ultimate rightness and goodness and truth of that spirit which lived and spoke within him.

Let us for a moment let our eye rove back over that appalling succession of mistakes and miseries which constitute the greater part of Shelley's worldly life. We see the persecution at Eton, the expulsion from Oxford, the break with his family, the Irish crusades, the Elizabeth Hitchener fiasco, the tragedy of Harriet, the verdict of the Chancery Court, and finally the flight from an England that was glad to be rid of him; and we see too, if we but take the small trouble of peering a bit beneath the surface, that all that was lamentable or culpable in him sprang solely and directly from his refusal to recognize any standard of value or conduct save his own. That his standard was incomparably higher than that of the society against which he pitted himself had little to do with the matter; his sin was not simply that he was "different," but that he was actively, militantly so. The poet once said of himself with perfect truth that in all his life he had never committed any act which he did not in his heart believe was right. Right as *he* saw it: that was the beginning and the end of morality. It is, no doubt, the noblest morality of all, but one which, in this world of adjustments and compromises, most of us find advisable to leave behind with pipe and slippers when we leave the philosophical fireside. Not so Shelley, for whom believing was doing. And so it happened that the inevitable irony of his life was that those deeds of his, which, judged by human social standards were the most reprehensible, were precisely those in which by his own standards he was acting most justly. He was expelled from Oxford because he would not purchase absolution at the price of his sincerity; he turned from the "Brown Demon" because he was incapable of paying false homage to a goddess in whom he no longer believed; and he left Harriet Westbrook for Mary Godwin for the insanely simple and irrefutable reason that he loved the one and did not love the other. He could conceive of no more hideous sin than living together without mutual love; the supreme evil was unquestioning allegiance to Custom without the endorsement of the individual spirit.

In the abstract this seems more the attitude of a god than of a man; in practice it proved to be the credo of a menace to society. All the unhappiness of Shelley's social life—and there was much of it—is attributable to his lack of what we call the "human touch"; he had sympathy immeasurable for the miseries of men, but he had none for their limitations and their weaknesses. He demanded too much of people, and when they were unable to meet his demands, both he and they suffered. He asked Harriet to understand—asked, indeed, a sixteen-year-old girl of orthodox training and moderate intelligence to cast off at one swipe the whole complex society and code of the world she knew, to trample under her feet all those things which she had been taught were good and worthy and desirable, to heed and to flaunt in the face of an outraged England an ideal of which she could not even conceive. Of everyone he expected that same high consecration to the Cause which made him unique among men, and he learned to his bitter sorrow that none could stand the pace. Mary Godwin, alone of all those who came into intimate spiritual contact with him, was able in a degree to meet the superhuman requirements which he set; if for no other reason, the daughter of William Godwin and Mary Wollstonecraft was a great woman in that she was a worthy and understanding mate to Percy Shelley. She was able to take him as he was. With others it was otherwise: with Harriet, who, after he had left her, wilted and went to pieces and ended in the Serpentine; with English society, which tolerated him just so long and then flicked him from her, as a great beast flicks from it an insistently pestiferous insect that is disturbing its rest; with his father and his mother and Miss Hitchener; with Oxford dons and Irish republicans and finally even with Hogg; with all people, individually and collectively, with whom he came in contact. And as he asked too much of men, so did he ask too much of the gods. The mortals could not—the immortals would not—oblige; for of them he demanded clarity and significance and answers to his questions, and

NOUMENON

these happen to be things of which the heavenly wardens are notoriously chary. Doubtless they smiled at his presumption, but perhaps their smile was touched with wonder. For Shelley went on. Untaught, untamed, and undismayed, he streamed through life and across the face of the earth, heeding a rampart no more than a grassblade, high of heart and strong of purpose; and somehow as time progresses, the débris he left behind him becomes ever less clear and less important. He was a misfit, then, among men, a presumptuous inquisitor before the gods, in that he asked too much of both. But perhaps it is only by asking that we may attain at last to our desire.

Most things—most men—we meet are too complex for our understanding; Shelley, on the other hand, is almost too simple. Scandalized philistines of his own day branded him a monster; later generations, well out of the danger-zone of his living personality, have sentimentalized him into angelhood; his reputation, in general, has varied between those of a rather foolish idealist and a rather idealistic fool. Shelley was a strange creature, but he was not "rather" anything; whatever he was, he was complete and whole of his kind. We have called him a child, but he did not possess the normal child's common sense and adaptability. Rather is he like a baby—a radiant, newborn creature, fresh from the Elsewhere, possessed, by some mystic process, of a vast store of knowledge and an unquenchable vital energy, but as yet untouched by any save the mother who bore him, still ignorant of his obligation of saying "ga" when nurse holds up two fingers and "goo" when she holds up three. The world never got its hooks into him, never taught him to see as it would have him see or react as it would have him react. The one great shibboleth which every infant is taught as he comes into life and which he never after forgets—the key to the conduct of all men in all situations—is to do "the expected," and this Shelley never learned at all. For him there was no distinction between those things which one might with propriety see and those things which one might not, between what was permissible in word and action and what was taboo; he snapped his fingers in the face of the accumulated tradition of centuries, renounced with iconoclastic fury the ageless divinities of Custom and Usage, and did homage to but one God: himself and the spirit that moved in him. With his eyes and his mind and his heart he experienced the world; he saw much that was beautiful and much that was ugly, and he responded in the only way he could. The unheard-of simplicity of the process is matched only by the unheard-of innocence of the spirit from which it took its being.

The word "innocence," largely because of its immemorial service in the jargon of soporific religions, has grown to have a bad connotation; at best it is considered a negative virtue, and in these super-civilized days of frenzied sophistication, education for all, and A.B.'s for almost all, it is practically synonymous with ignorance. Shelley's innocence was of a slightly different genre. His mind, when he was called upon to play at wits, was as subtle as a sophist's, his emotional experience as deep—if perforce less broad—as that of the octogenarian Goethe; throughout his life, as he wrote of himself, and wrote with perfect truth, he "incessantly speculated, thought, and read." The antithesis of his innocence is not sophistication but prostitution, not the worldly shrug of the shoulder that comes with dubious wisdom but the far worse sin, the cardinal sin, of the outright corruption of man's most precious birthright. He came into the world pure—militantly pure—and his lifelong battle was with those who could rob him of his purity and leave in its place the world's ever-ready substitute of comfortable whitewash. One cannot help comparing him with Caspar Hauser, that mysterious man-child who appeared a decade after Shelley's death in the German city of Nürnberg and whose brief stay among men remains perhaps the bitterest single indictment which modern society has generated against its own structure. Both were possessed of an other-worldly simplicity of spirit which made them unique and unclassifiable in the societies into which they came; both were innocent to a degree that rendered them misfits in a complex, highly institutionalized civilization. They were not cogs in the social machine; they were individuals—wide-eyed, questioning, elemental individuals —who had not learned the great lesson of taking things for granted. The world made short work of Hauser, who in his passive naïveté was all too easy a mark for any and all who would take advantage of him. It found a harder nut to crack in Shelley. For in him it met a spirit who, far from being plastic or static, was as firm and as passionately alive as a meteor, who bore his integrity of soul not quietly, deep within him as a refuge, but proudly upon his lance-head as a challenge, who, with the full consciousness of what he was doing and with a tremendous reservoir of knowledge and intellectual truth from which to draw, not only considered it his right but his most sacred duty to rebel against the order of the earth. We should pity Hauser, but we should not pity Shelley. For whereas the one was a test for man, the other was his inquisitor; whereas one was a slaughtered lamb, the other was a warrior high of heart. Shelley fought with his eyes open: he knew that he demanded more than could be granted him and that in pitting his individuality against the enormous communality of society he must of necessity receive blow for blow and suffer in defeat even as he soared in victory. "We live on," he once wrote, "and in living lose the apprehension of life." He himself refused to lose it. The price he paid was terrific, but he succeeded in maintaining "that inner sanctity of soul" which to him was the one, the only, good in life. With innocent simplicity he came into the world and with innocent simplicity he left it. Its preservation was his greatest struggle and his greatest victory.

Whether or not we judge the game to be worth the candle depends upon whether we look at him primarily as a symbol of abstract human personality or as a social unit in a social whole. If we think of drowned Harriet, he was wretchedly wrong; if we think of "Prometheus Unbound," he was gloriously right. In the company of those wise and mature thinkers who have believed that the great goal of humankind is happiness on earth he is not fit to hold up his head; in the procession before the judgment-throne, in which each spirit who would enter the Kingdom of Heaven is bidden to come "simply, as a little child," he stands first of all men. Each of us must judge him by his own weights and measures. Or, if we happen to be more wise than human, we will refrain from judging him at all.

Prophet

> "Be through my lips to unawakened earth
> The trumpet of a prophecy! O Wind,
> If Winter comes, can Spring be far behind?"

It is a dangerous practice, albeit an almost universal one, to classify Shelley among the romantic poets. He possesses their verve, their fire, their love of individual freedom in the fullest measure, and his song, like that of Keats and Coleridge and Wordsworth, is not the expression of a code or tradition but of spontaneous personal feeling; in his interests, however, and in his attitude toward life he is utterly unlike them. The touchstone of true romanticism, we have pointed out, is the love of "the thing" for its own sake; it is aesthetic, pagan, anti-intellectual in its very essence; and in its pure form, as in the verse of Keats and Robert Frost, is concerned not at all either with wordly conditions in particular or with social and moral problems in general. How different from this is the spirit which manifests itself in flaming life in almost every line that Shelley ever wrote. A pagan only insofar as he refused to accept the hand-me-down theology of a church that had long outlived its significance, he was in a far deeper sense the most passionately unshakable of believers. An anti-intellectual in his conviction that intuitive imagination and not formed reason should be recognized as the last court of appeal of the human soul, the whole structure of his creed was yet founded upon that rock-bottom of intellectualism which is so foreign to the romantics. And finally, although his hierophancy to the divinity of beauty is not merely factual but proverbial, it would be little less than blasphemy to foist upon him the aesthete's creed of art for art's dear sake. A true romanticist turns his back upon the flux of the living world; Shelley did not merely not turn his back, he plunged headforemost into the maelstrom, and the wonder is that he was not crushed to death. A true romanticist renounces transient imperfection in his consecration to the eternally abiding perfection; Shelley renounced nothing. He asked questions, he demanded answers, he prayed that his poetry might be not only a thing of lasting, static beauty, but "the trumpet of a prophecy." It is here that we strike upon his most fundamental difference from his contemporaries in English verse. Whereas their attitude toward life was objective, "appreciative," his was subjective, passionately partisan, hortatory. Whereas they loved the "thing," he loved the "idea." Whereas they were simply poets, he was a prophet besides.

It is a fashion of this emancipated twentieth century of ours to admit the follies and failings of our really rather unimportant little earth and to suggest urbanely that nothing very much can be done about them. Reporting is our demand in literature, "impartial artistry" is the thing, and so fanatically partial a crusader as Shelley is in danger of being relegated to that dubiously loud-mouthed brotherhood of reformers wherein John Wesley and Anthony Comstock are the standard-bearers. For did he not himself confess that he had "a passion for reforming the world?" Assuredly he did; but it is well also to remember that he wrote that "didactic poetry is my abhorrence." Always it must be remembered of him that he cared less about men than about Man and that his appeal was directed not primarily toward society but toward the individual spirits who composed that society. His challenge was not rational, but spiritual, not a futile, obnoxious harangue on the desirability of being other than what we are, but a plea that we recognize and assert the highest potentialities that are in us. And—most significant of all in our understanding of him—he spoke as he did, not primarily because thereby mankind would be improved but because it was *in* him to speak thus. He was a crusader in word and act because he was a crusader in spirit. He was clear-sighted enough to see the topless

NOUMENON

pyramid of evil and injustice which men have raised upon the earth, and he was child enough, madman enough (call it what you will) not to hold his tongue about what he saw. We do not need Shelley to tell us *ex cathedra* of his mission, for few things are more obvious than that he found the world a rather imperfect place. Throughout his poetry stalked the torturing, inescapable knowledge that man is honeycombed with cruelty and deceit and meanness and fear, and the earth with pain and ugliness and death, and throughout, too, there flames the affirmation that this should not be so. This was no armchair philosopher, secure in the comfortable panacea of a "system," or supersensitive blinding to swathe the misery of earth in a rosy optimism; this was no appreciative extrovert, a passive receptacle for impressions; this was no rationalist to lose sight of man in his quest of abstract truth, no well fed "objective realist" to go a-slumming and mumble of inevitabilities; for better or worse, this was not the man who could take things as they came. This was Shelley, drunk with beauty and with the glory of which he had had a vision, recognizing evil, hating it, fighting it. He could not ignore the world, as did Keats; he could not flee it, as did Wordsworth and Tennyson and Arnold; he could not accept and embrace it, as did Goethe. And so he fought it. Never did he descend to preaching and didacticism, but never, either, did he bow before the great "whatever-is." For in his heart was the desire to have the earth and the things and the men of the earth not as they are but as they ought to be—as he knew that on some far day they could be; and in the grip of that desire he could neither rest nor turn aside nor acquiesce. The madness of prophecy was upon him; and the vision which he held before him was the unending perfectibility of man.

MAD SHELLEY

Since that long-gone day when the great hierarchy of Judah came to an end, the world has not dealt kindly with these who have set themselves up as its prophets. Cassandra had a hard life. So did Jesus and John Hus and Jeanne D'Arc and Galileo and Leon Trotzky. So did Shelley. Friedrich Hebbel, the great German dramatist, was pointing toward such as these when he gave his warning: "Nur rühre nimmer an den Schlaf der Welt." The sleep of the world. . . . It is bad policy for wide-eyed little Johnny to pull on papa's sleeve while he is enjoying his post-business snooze for no better reason than that the sun is shining brightly and it seems to his immature judgment a shame to snore the time away. If papa is awakened he is apt to be annoyed at his child, for his sleep is precious to him. So is the world's sleep to the world, and mature minds from Plato to Stalin have ever recognized that it is better undisturbed. They have dealt summarily with prophets—with those innocent, much-demanding children who, in their consecration to their Cause, have been unable, or unwilling, to see that all the world is not so young as they. From the beginning Shelley played the prophet; from the beginning he matched his vision against the massed reality of tradition and accepted fact. And he suffered for his foolishness. In England his life was one protracted succession of bitter disappointments and defeats, a cumulative proof of his impotence in the face of all that he so passionately believed to be wrong. We have already sketched in brief his disastrous relations both with society and with individuals; his expulsion from Oxford, his break with his family, the fiasco of Elizabeth, the tragedy of Harriet, the final hegira from the homeland. In those early days of fanatical discipleship to Freedom, he liked to think of himself more as a champion of social and political reform than as an imaginative singer; he had not yet attained to that perfect clarity of insight through which he was later to see that his true rôle was not that of a practical but of a spiritual liberator. The flame of his own spontaneous spirit had found fuel in the doctrines of the French and English radicals, and, armed with their zealot's creed of social meliorism, he flung himself with the heedless innocence of a child upon the massed evil of the world. The masters at whose feet he sat were earnest, rationalistic thinkers with nothing of the poet about them—least of all William Godwin, whose coldly factual "Political Justice" seems a strange bible for that young spirit who was later to grow into the purest lyrist of his age. The early Shelley believed himself to be prophet and reformer first and last and poet only incidentally, because he believed he *ought* so to be; in no man who has ever appeared on earth did that "categorical imperative" of which Kant spoke manifest itself more strongly or lead to more wildly outlandish deeds than in that incredibly naïve bolshevik of eighteen years who on a March morning in the year 1811 set out— by request—from Oxford to reform the world.

Shelley's adventures and misadventures in his seven-year struggle with English society are too numerous, as they are too well known, to dwell on at length. He could no more resist attacking what he believed to be evil than a bull can resist charging a red rag. Crusade followed crusade, all of them undertaken with prophetic zeal, all of them carried through with holy integrity of purpose to their ultimate—and almost invariably disastrous —conclusions. He married Harriet, less because he wanted to than because he believed it to be his duty to rescue her from the real or imagined oppression of her parents;

he voyaged twice to Ireland and confounded the hard-headed Dublin politicians with his abstract chatter on the inanity of formal religion; he threw himself with the unbounded altruistic energy of the centenarian Faust into a Mr. Maddock's plan for reclaiming an area of swampland near Tremadoc, in Wales; under the influence of his friends, the Newtons, he became an ardent vegetarian, and an amusing anecdote is told of his interpretation of the vultures in the Prometheus myth as the spirit of indigestion gnawing at the vitals of meat-eating man. Enthusiasm was unbounded, tact and restraint non-existent; Godwin himself, from whom Shelley had first lit the torch which he now bore aloft, grew apprehensive of this mad disciple who had grown so out of hand, and warned him that he was "preparing a scene of blood!" But the mad disciple continued on his path, and that unheeding spirit which had, in adolescence, produced the abortive battle-cries of "Zastrozzi" and "The Wandering Jew," "Margaret Nicholson" and "The Defense of Atheism" went on, in young manhood, to the creation of "Queen Mab." This poem, his first of importance, fairly embodies the content and attitude of Shelley's mind from his eighteenth to his twenty-first year and marks the apogee of his devotion to the cause of social reform. In it he speaks for the last time rather as a reformer than as a poet, rather as a meliorist than an idealist; it incorporates once and for all those social and political ideas which were later to be subordinated to the growing force of more imaginative vision. The best summation of the spirit that lay behind "Queen Mab" is, as usual, Mrs. Shelley's. "He was animated," she writes, "to greater zeal by compassion for his fellow creatures. His sympathy was excited by the misery with which the world

NOUMENON

is bursting. He witnessed the sufferings of the poor, and was aware of the evils of ignorance. He desired to induce every rich man to despoil himself of superfluity, and to create a brotherhood of property and service, and was ready to be the first to lay down the advantages of his birth. . . . He did not in his youth look forward to gradual improvement; nay, in those days of intolerance, now almost forgotten, it seemed as easy to look forward to the sort of millennium of freedom and brotherhood, which he thought the proper state of mankind, as to the present reign of moderation and improvement. . . . He saw, in a fervent call on his fellow creatures to share alike the blessings of the creator, to love and serve each other, the noblest work that life and time permitted him. In this spirit he composed 'Queen Mab.' "

And in this spirit, let it not be forgotten, he composed every subsequent line that he ever wrote. For Shelley grew, but he did not change. Wisdom came with age and with those miserable years in which he lost Harriet, then his children, and finally his native homeland altogether; and the child who had tried to speak with the voice of a man became the man who saw with the eyes of a child. He outgrew those mentors whose creed of red revolt he had sought to carry to extreme fulfilment; his approach thereafter to the problems of the world was never practical, but always imaginative. The reformer became the prophet, but the fundamental spirit of which both were simply different aspects remained untouched by all that time and circumstance could do, and while after 1816 there were no more "Declarations of Rights" or invasions of Ireland or fleets of propaganda-freighted bottles, the flame of his belief in the rightness and beauty of his Cause, far from weakening, grew brighter and stronger with the years. It is a far cry from the almost hysterical assertiveness of "Queen Mab" to the melancholy brooding of "Alastor," which of all Shelley's poems is nearest in spirit to the true romantic verse of Wordsworth and Coleridge. In its every line is apparent the deepening and refining of his consciousness which three years of suffering and of living almost constantly in the shadow of death had effected: the tone is quieter, richer, more profound; now, we realize, we are listening to a man who is facing not merely the traditions and institutions of a passing world but the infinitely more awesome antagonist of his own soul. But that soul he faced was unchanged from of old. He still saw with the same eyes, thought with the same mind, felt with the same heart, still could perceive that

> ". . . Heartless things
> Are done and said i' the world, and many worms
> And beasts and men live on. . . ."

and still affirmed that these things should not be so. Oh no, Shelley the Red had by no means been tamed. In "Laon and Cythna," the longest and most ideologically comprehensive of his poems, his imaginatively idealized brother-and-sister lovers proved too much for fastidious England to stomach, and he was compelled to bowdlerize it to a considerable extent before it was published in its final form as "The Revolt of Islam." His bitter complaints at the necessity of revision were probably founded more on principle than on actual grievance, for the finished product was one of which even so merciless a self-critic as he could not have failed to be proud. As Byronism is epitomized in "Don Juan," so is Shelleyism in "The Revolt of Islam." It is quite simply, to use its creator's own words, "a tale of passionate change," and

NOUMENON

remains as the most complete revelation of Shelley's philosophy of life and vision of the future, as it is also, with "Paradise Lost," the most grandly conceived and executed narrative poem in the English language. Written at Great Marlow in the summer of 1817, it was his valedictory to his homeland and his final, perfect expression of the spiritual victory which he had won in his unending struggle with her ways. In those years of misery, ill health, and universal condemnation a poet had been born, but a prophet had not died. Rather had he grown to magnificent stature.

And so did the prophet continue and grow stronger in Italian exile, for Shelley—however much he may after have wished to do so—could never shake off the consciousness that just beyond the horizon of his quiet, sheltered life there stretched a boundless world of pain and oppression and wrong. He could not be convinced that "The Cenci," generally considered the greatest English tragedy since Shakespeare, amounted to very much, for the simple reason that there was not very much of himself in it; it did not touch upon those ideas and ideals which for him were the beginning and the end of artistic creation, even as they were of life, and it gave him, he declared, "less trouble than anything I have written of the same length." There was beauty in "The Cenci," splendid poetry, dramatic action; but there was no prophecy, no call to arms. It was not written with Shelley's lifeblood as were "Prometheus" and "Adonais" and his great odes "To the Skylark" and "To the West Wind," in which every word and every image is whipped into higher and more intense life by the driving power of his Cause. To the very end he retained his "passion for reforming the world" and exercised his inalienable prerogative of recognizing evil where he saw it, of hating it, of denouncing it. In his noblest verse he rose far above the particular and the worldly into the sphere of the pure ideal, but he never scorned stooping to direct attack when he believed attack was merited. In "Oedipus" and "Peter Bell the Third" he approached the nearest that he ever came to satire in his heartfelt ridicule of the English *mores*, nor was the old "conscientious objector" of Eton, Oxford and the British Isles at large so far smothered in the lyric poet but that he could rise to the occasion of the notorious Peterloo Massacre of 1819 with the impassioned battle-call of "The Mask of Anarchy." "Hellas," best of all his later poems, exhibits that process of the idealization of reality which is so typical of Shelley, for it is, on the one hand, far more a work of art than his outright political verses and, on the other, more close to the earth than the highly spiritualized rhapsodies of his greatest masterpieces. In it we can see perhaps more clearly than elsewhere the fundamental relationship between the humanist and the individualist which together composed his unified nature, and attain to a measure of understanding of the man who within the space of less than one year could, in "The Witch of Atlas," soar to the most etherealized exquisiteness of personal fancy, and in the closing stanza of "The Mask of Anarchy," write lines which might well supplant the "Internationale" as the battle-hymn of modern Communism. For the romantic singer who dreamed of eyes as deep "as are two openings of unfathomable night seen through a temple's cloven roof" is indeed the selfsame man as that intensely social-minded young disciple of the French Revolution who bade the men of England:

NOUMENON

> "Rise like lions after slumber
> In unvanquishable number!
> Shake your chains to earth, like dew
> Which in sleep had fallen on you—
> Ye are many, they are few!"

With the coming of artistic wisdom and mature apprehension of the true nature of his Cause, Shelley, naturally enough, grew far beyond his early self, and in his later years expressed no uncertain disapproval of such a mad, inchoate effusion of his prophetic infancy as "Queen Mab." It outraged his sense of the transcendental mission of poetry, just as "Götz" and "Werther" outraged the more Olympian creator of "Iphigenie" and the Second Part of "Faust"; for he, like Goethe, had won with the years to a universal idealism from the enormous elevation of which his early, puerilely purposeful outbursts could not but appear ridiculous. But, however much he deplored its taste and form, its basic spirit still rejoiced his constant heart. In 1817, after admitting "Queen Mab" to be "full of those errors which belong to youth," he made it not only his confession but his boast that his devotion to the doctrines therein expressed had in no respect diminished or wavered. Writing to his publisher in 1821, he was much harsher with the poem, but even then, a scant year before his death, his disapproval was founded not upon any of its articles of faith but upon its crudity of expression, which he feared rendered the whole "better fitted to injure than to serve the sacred cause of freedom." At Casa Magni Shelley was playing upon a different instrument from that of Poland Street and Cwm Elan— an instrument of richer, fuller tone and infinitely greater depth of feeling—but he was playing still to the same old tune. "The Triumph of Life," in the composition of which he was overtaken by his death, was planned on the same grand scale and in substantially the same key as "The Revolt of Islam"; the prophet who lay in his shallop as it drifted among the sheltered coves of the Gulf of Spezzia, and wrote of blood and gold, of Rousseau and Napoleon, was the same prophet who had stood alone and weakly miserable in the yard of Eton College and had sworn his magnificently childish oath of lifelong consecration. In his heart he had neither changed, nor faltered, nor repented; the clothing of his prophecy had become richer and more splendid with the years, but the living spirit which moved within the crucible of art was borne intact and inviolate from womb to grave. It manifested itself no less in his adolescent monstrosities than in the most perfect masterpieces of his ripest years, and no less in his life than in his meditations and writings; it was the living force behind the boyish insanity of the "Defense of Atheism" and the marriage with Harriet and the Irish pilgrimages, as it was behind the consummate artistry of "Prometheus Unbound"; it impelled him to almost every line he ever wrote and every act he ever performed, and in the grip of its inspiration the medium through whom it sang seems less a man than "the trumpet of a prophecy" which he desired and believed himself to be. That spirit was Freedom. And Shelley the Prophet, whether at a given moment he happened to be engaged in remonstrating with Mr. Bethel of Eton on the injustice of the fagging system, or in haranguing a mob of good Irish-Catholic Dubliners on the desirability of atheism, or in composing the final apocalyptic utterance of Demogorgon, was Shelley the Liberator. It was so, not occasionally, not sporadically at his highest moments, but always throughout his life. In the "Hymn to Intellectual Beauty," written in 1816, he speaks thus to the spirit which he served:

> "I vowed that I would dedicate my powers
> To thee and thine—have I not kept the vow?"

He could have asked the question at any time during his twenty-five years of conscious life, and the answer—if the spirit deigned to answer—would always have been the same.

Poet

It is well-nigh impossible in the tightly woven fabric of Shelley's nature to distinguish where the prophet ends and where the poet begins. He himself was so vividly aware of the indivisible oneness of the didactic and the artistic elements of his spirit that he repudiated as true products of his spirit any creation in which both did not appear in fullest measure, and he recognized—as the world, by a considerably less spontaneous process, has since also recognized—that his greatest achievements were those in which poetry and prophecy were blended into most harmonious unity. He could not, on the one hand, sing a note without striving to fit it into his philosophical scale, nor, on the other, could he contemplate the serious problems of the world without bursting into song. There are "blood and gold" and "sleeping priests, all of one sort" in "The Witch of Atlas" and "stars [which] from Night's loose hair are shaken" in "The Mask of Anarchy." Shelley could soar lyrically high into realms which no other poet has ever trod, but he could never wholly forget the rolling earth beneath and the magnificently pitiful creatures who crawled upon its crust; and he could plumb the most abysmal depths of human ugliness and misery, but never without perceiving in every puddle and sewer upon which he came the reflected vision of the stars. In many of his poems (as, for example, in the two just mentioned) art and purpose, while almost perfectly commingled, cannot be called truly one: in "The Witch of Atlas" the true poet of the fancy is predominant, and the objective reader cannot but feel that the allusions to social conditions are a bit extraneous; and in "The Mask of Anarchy" the reverse is the case. Prophet and poet are so fundamentally inextricable in Shelley that we instinctively feel something to be amiss when they become in the least distinguishable in his verse, and we adjudge those creations of his to be the noblest in which they are as inseparable as in the man himself. "The Revolt of Islam," "Adonais," "Ode to the West Wind," "Hellas," and above all "Prometheus": these are the poems in which we perceive the spirit of their maker, not only clearly, but whole. And to perceive Shelley other than whole is scarcely to see him at all.

The name "philosophical poetry," with its attendant implications of sobriety and passionless contemplation, may seem a ridiculous tag to hang onto Shelley's verse, but it is nevertheless an inevitable one; for if Shelley, on the one hand, was the foremost example of rampant individualism which his age produced, he is none the less, on the other, the most self-consciously systematic thinker in the long galaxy of English poets. In the preface to "Prometheus" he indicates his position as follows: "Should I live to accomplish what I propose, that is, produce a systematical history of what appear to me to be the genuine elements of human society, let not the advocates of injustice and superstition flatter themselves that I should take Aeschylus rather than Plato as my model." Or, in other words, he proposes to build his magic structure of

NOUMENON

transcendent song upon the rock-bottom of intellectual theory and to weave the evanescent substances of his dreams into the abiding oneness of The Dream. In another poet this attitude would be disastrous to spontaneous imagination; in him it was the first essential of art. He needed direction, he needed a central motivating force about which he might drape his richly brilliant pattern of words and images; without them he would have been as aimless as a planet without an orbit and a sun. He could not, as could Keats, seize upon one particular province and make it his own without asking questions about other possibly important provinces, nor could he, like Shakespeare, survey them all and ask no questions either. The romanticist looks at "the thing in itself," the objective realist at "things in general," and neither is much given to philosophizing over what he sees. Shelley, on the contrary, was bitten by the metaphysical bug, and was bitten hard. In his early youth, as we have mentioned, he did not know whether his path lay primarily along intellectual or imaginative lines, for simultaneously he felt within him the compelling urge to sing and the equally compelling urge to ask of life a million-and-one unanswerable questions which do not, at first hearing, sound very compatible with song. But in the end they were compatible. For in Shelley, more than any other man except Goethe, song and thought were one, and, as he grew in years and wisdom, this fact became more clear and exhibited itself both in the unique comprehensiveness of his ripest verse and in the unique comprehensiveness of his own personality. He brought to poetry the indefatigable mind of a philosopher, to philosophy the untrammelled spirit of a poet, and in the combination he was spared the heaviness of the one and the limitation of the other. Surely enough he could not be the master in every field into which his vast spirit carried him: he was not so profound as Kant nor so exquisite an interpreter of the senses as Keats, and he lacked in a great measure (though by no means so completely as is generally believed) the worldly sense of Goethe and Shakespeare. But in that magnificently universal field which he made primarily his own, in which thought and feeling, intellect and imagination, poetry and philosophy fuse into flaming unity of spirit, he is supreme. Not only is he alone in stature; he is alone in kind.

Perhaps the most eloquent tribute to the scope of Shelley's genius is contained in the fact that the pure poet in him was stifled not one whit by his devotion to a Cause, and that in his absorption in the Ideal he attained at the same time to a well-nigh perfect mastery of those sensuous images which, after all, are the true brick and mortar of every poet's edifice. Into whatever undreamed demi-worlds of moonlight and music and feeling his earth-scorning spirit might carry him, he began his flights always from the solid ground of clear-eyed observation, and the process by which he developed his images from original perception to final imaginative symbolism was invariably the same: the idealization of the real. "The mist of familiarity," he wrote, "obscures from us the wonder of our being." Men cannot feel greatly because they cannot see clearly, and they cannot see clearly because their vision is obscured by custom and by the accepted standards which civilization has imposed upon them no less in the operation of their senses than in that of their minds. As the mission of prophecy is to liberate the intellect, so is that of poetry to liberate the perception, in that "it strips the veil of familiarity from the world, and lays bare the naked and sleeping beauty, which is the spirit of its forms." These words,

NOUMENON

perhaps, in their almost perfect expression of the credo of romanticism, may at first hearing seem strange in the mouth of so unshakable an intellectualist as Shelley. What must be remembered is that this attitude is the starting-point and not the sum and circumference of Shelley's march: he looked at "things" partly, indeed, for their own sake, but partly, too, even preeminently, that by perceiving them imaginatively he might pass through them to that which lay beyond; the spirits and the forms of the world were in their deepest sense but sign-posts pointing toward the one Spirit and the one Form of which they were but the transient reflexes. He used his senses to their utmost, but he could not stop with what they gave him; and, while he could contemplate "the thing" with the intense joy of discerning, childlike vision, he had also the child's insatiable desire to discover "how it works." The fact is simply that there *was* no sum or circumference of Shelley's march: one victory was the trumpet which called to a new struggle; one divinely intuitive perception was not to be accepted at its own worth but woven into a greater fabric. The ladder which he climbed was pitched against an ever-receding star, and beyond each rung attained there appeared another yet to be won.

And thus it is that in Shelley's poetry the sensuous stuff of the world is seldom self-sufficient, but is almost invariably incorporated into an endless succession of greater and yet greater concepts. Going to nature he found beauty but never that beauty which is one with truth and which "is all ye know on earth, and all ye need to know." Even in the last days of calmly wise maturity, when, far distant both in miles and years from the noisy hysteria of his first passionate *libertad*, he walked and mused in a glamorous picture-world whose form was wrought of laurel groves and sleeping marble and whose spirit was the warm, vagrant breath of the sirocco, he could never forget that all the loveliness of which his senses drank was less reality than a symbol of reality. Nature, for nature's sake alone, was for him less a positive divinity to be worshipped and adored than a negative refuge from the storms of the world-spirit. "In solitude," he wrote, "or in that deserted state when we are surrounded by human beings, and yet they sympathize not with us, we love the flowers, the grass, and the waters, and the sky." These were his loves on those rare occasions when he turned his spirit from mankind— when the one Love of his life became a cross too great for him to bear. The infinite manifestations of nature were for him an escape and an anodyne in his transient periods of weakness; in his abiding strength they were the means to an end, the path on which he trod in his unending quest; but not the goal itself.

Founding his assertion largely on this basically unromantic attitude toward the phenomena of the material world, Professor Whitehead has recently departed so far from the Arnold-Thompson-Maurois tradition of "Arielism" as to suggest that Shelley, if alive today, would rank as a Newton among chemists. In support of this hypothesis he cites the usual passages which have always been referred to in proof of the poet's firm grasp of scientific fact: "the sapless foliage of the ocean," "the vaporous exultation not to be confined," the dead leaves of autumn "like ghosts from an enchanter fleeing," the cloud which "changes but cannot die"; and so on. That Shelley was a remarkably accurate observer of physical phenomena is undeniable. To science, as to rationalistic philosophy, he brought his immense power of perception and assimilation, but to both he brought also the transmuting spirit of

NOUMENON

his own personality which in the end left him wholly content with neither. He had, at one and the same time, Newton's passion for relationships and Hume's scepticism of the very existence of what we call cause and effect, the chemist's microscopic eye for the fact and the metaphysician's nose for the abstract; he always began his flights from the earthly empiricism of the former but he always ended in the latter's empyrean of the Ideal, and in his position between the two he can properly neither be called one nor the other. Shelley knew facts but he did not reverence them as the end of all search: mathematics ran second only to history in the repulsion which it aroused in him, and the half-chemical, half-alchemical experiments with which he scared Bethel half to death and supplied picturesque material for Hogg's descriptive pen, while admittedly disclosing a mind prone to ask questions of the material world, were undertaken not in the abstract spirit of investigation but in the passionate spirit of adventure. Whitehead makes the usual mistake of taking one aspect of Shelley for the whole; in contemplating the mind which seized upon every known law of the material-mechanical universe as food for its endless machinations, he forgets that greater comprehensive spirit which would no more have rested content with a foolproof formula than with a well-turned image or a syllogism. Shelley did possess a strong sense of the organic unity of nature: he was as fond as Goethe of the word "weave" to express those perceptible processes which he intuitively felt to be but phases of the Process, and his cosmology, as developed in "Prometheus," is founded upon a concept of successive growth and decay and regrowth which a century of research has wholly supported. He knew the earth for the geologist's spinning parcel of mass and pressure, but he knew it also

—and knew it best—as that ungeologically articulate spirit who hears and feels the Titan's kiss along its marble nerves, who is the giver and the taker away, the sower and reaper, the sown and the reaped,

> —"Who takes the life she gave, even as a mother,
> Folding her child, says, 'Leave me not again.'"

Whitehead recognizes that Shelley could never conceive of a nature divorced from its aesthetic values. He should go a step farther and say rather "spiritual values." Insofar as science is an approach to the nature of the living organism of the universe and an attempt to integrate its infinitely various parts into harmonious, meaningful unity, Shelley is foremost among its prophets; but to its enforced method of earth-grubbing empiricism and to its watchword of "disinterested observation" he is utterly alien.

Another rôle which has been more or less foisted upon Shelley in an attempt to explain his attitude and his standard of reality is that of mystic. Biographers and critics from Hogg to Maurois have almost without exception been impressed by the strange "otherworldliness" of their subject and have tried, with varying degrees of success, to interpret it psychologically as the manifestation of this or that quality of mind; such men as the poet, Francis Thompson, and the modern psychologist, George Barnefield, have chosen to use the word "mysticism." There is, indeed, no lack of proof that the poet's mental and nervous processes were different from those of the normal man: in the first place, there are the nocturnal assassin of Tanyrallt, the lovesick lady of Naples, and the outrageous assaulter of the Pisan post-office—all personages whose actual existence is more than dubious;

then, too, it is definitely known that he was visited by nightmares and suffered from waking hallucinations of tremendous intensity; add to all this his almost continual state of physical ill-health, his taking of laudanum to soothe his nerves, his susceptibility to the minutest stimuli, and, finally, his own repeatedly affirmed feeling of a force that moved within him and was yet not he, and one has sufficient evidence for the average man that he was not far from insanity. Or, if insanity is too harsh a word, the vaguely inclusive cloak of mysticism will fit him nicely. Thus reason those observers who have concentrated their attention upon the irrational in Shelley's nature, forgetting that in his other aspects he is, variously, no less a fact-scenting scientist, a systematic metaphysician, and a street-corner political agitator. There is much that is mystical in him, just as there is much that is intellectual, and neither can be divorced from the other without the attendant disintegration of that personality in which they existed as one. In his relation to the universal, in his almost oriental sense of the cosmic rhythm which breathes its being into the essence of all created things and in his conviction of the utter meaninglessness of death, he appears as a mystic; in his attitude to the affairs of earth and earthly men he is not only a theoretical, but a militant, humanist. The transcendental sage who in his wisdom knew that life, in all its transient pomp, is no more than a stain upon the white radiance of the abiding All was also the outraged young man, who, one stormy winter night at Marlow, found a wretched old charwoman lying upon the road in fits and warned the comfortable householder who refused to shelter her that for his callousness of heart, when the approaching revolution of the world-proletariat arrived, he would have his house burned over his head. If we are to accept Shelley as a mystic it must be with the same grain of salt with which we take him in any other arbitrary category. He was no more like William Blake than he was like Immanuel Kant or William Godwin. Mysticism is a soporific to the intellect, a negation of the significance of earthly life. It is passively anti-individualistic in its subordination of the ego to the universal tempo, and static in its acquiescence to the almighty Will. The author of "Prometheus Unbound" is a wee bit out of place beneath its sheltering wings.

Shelley liked to think of himself, and posterity has liked to think of him, as Ariel, and the unfortunate result is the all too prevalent impression of a sweet, if eccentric, skylark sporting through the upper air and flooding the heavens with melody, while earth sweats and moulders below in its casket of clouds. This is undoubtedly what the pure singing poet in him desired to be, but also undoubtedly what he in his united entirety was not. Wordsworth, in his later years, was able to forsake a half-witted and fuming world for mild and untroubling devotions to pantheism and celandines, Coleridge to pull on his pipe and dream gaudy visions of Xanadu, Keats to grasp for classic beauty and watch a civilization fall, unmoved. Shelley was built otherwise. Does Ariel sing of incest and of murder and of the Peterloo Massacre? Is Ariel thrown out of college for being an undesirable character and, more subtly, but no less surely, out of England for the same reason? Does he voyage twice to Ireland in the cause of revolt and fling fiery words at a street-gathering of malcontents? Does not Ariel mock and smile at the foibles and sorrows of earthbound men? Is he not happy, joyous, free? This is not Shelley—this is not he who above all men was born to feel the misery of earth and withal to rise above it in a song of defiance and affirmation. Rather is he to be likened to his own Prometheus, long-enduring and undismayed, loving life and loving that sacred liberty of spirit without which life is but a shadow and a mockery, who, chained to earth and with the Furies tearing at his entrails, could yet sing and aspire and thumb his nose at the immortal gods.

Shelley saw too clearly and felt too deeply to be either quite an Ariel or quite a mortal. Around him, above, below and within him, swayed a universe; beneath his feet rolled the timeless earth, the womb and the grave of men, a mute, impenetrable cosmos of rock and fire and water and life; before his eyes swam a meaningless panorama of blood and bondage and pain, of hard-eyed victory and dull-eyed defeat; and within his heart was that which told of something else, which shook and wilted at the touch of earth, which must find where it might the beauty and the love and the significance that is withheld from men. He was not constructed to be an appreciative extrovert, a passive receptacle for impressions. He could not find lasting joy in the song of a bird or in the choral of the wind for their own sakes; he could not thrill to the chiselled perfection of an Attic urn or to the tiny miracle of a flower and feel that here was beauty and here was truth and that nothing else mattered. For something else did matter. Vase and skylark and mountain fastness were all very well in their quiet way and would submit passively and unobstreperously to poetic idealization; but surely beauty and truth are harder won than this in a world wherein are hatred and ignorance and human pain, surely there is no perfection while the guillotine is whining and slaves are sweating and questions are unanswered, surely we are far from God if in the face of the boundless challenge of earth and heaven man can still deny his birthright and root his snout into the mud. Shelley was above all things a humanist and a humanitarian, and his song is ever the song of man. Outraged and appalled by the grossness of earth he would flee to the refuge of woodland, songbird, and rainbow, but his Furies followed in his train and the cry of undelivered man pursued him from the world he sought to—but could not—escape. His skylark is an asbestinized Icarus, his west-wind is the voice of Prometheus, the spirit that he serves is not one of achieved consummation but of endlessly progressive aspiration, and the song that he sings is not of appreciation but of desire.

Time and again he would try his wings and soar on the magic of his words and his imagination to a world of transcendent beauty; for beauty he could find, but never without pain. The aziola's cry is one of sadness; the voice of Jane, carried into the night on the tinkling of a guitar, sings of "a world far from ours," of a world unattainable; the trunkless legs of stone which stand in the waste speak not of that which was and is forever, but of that which was and shall not be again. In the art and the spirit of ancient Greece, Keats found sufficiency and perfection, and felt, as only the artist can feel, that here was flawless beauty and something complete in itself, which neither time nor change nor death of men could ever take away. Shelley could not thus be absorbed into the reality of one moment or one creation; he could not stand before the Venus de Milo or the Apollo Belvedere and say to his soul that "here is all ye know on earth, and all ye need to know"; he could not find in Homer or Phidias or Sophocles or any of the long-dead great that which others found or seemed to find. Here was beauty—yes. But here too, in the contained and august purity of the Parthenon as in the unquiet, earth-scorning upsweep of Cologne Cathedral, was incompleteness and ultimate frustration; here too was the old pain-wrung affirmation of beauty and significance; here too, in a land two thousand miles and two thousand years away, were the heavens aloof and silent and the immortals jealous of their secret. It was not in attainment of any particular goal but in undaunted struggle toward the Universal Goal that he lived and sang. He knew that his questionings would not be graciously answered, he knew that his pain would not be assuaged or his desires fulfilled, but he knew also, as did he before him who froze and bled upon a rock in the Caucasus, that the game was worth the candle; for in aspiration and in steadfast integrity of spirit and in the will of man to lift himself from his mud and chains up to the table of the gods he saw a majesty and a greatness of heart that all eternity could never dim. This is the song of a Titan and not of a sprite.

Small wonder then that Shelley's "sweetest songs are those that tell of saddest thoughts"; small wonder that at his greatest heights pain and exaltation mingle into oneness and into a power and splendor that is unmatched in any poetry, and that he to whom it was given to know both the most high and most deep should sing, above all others, of pain and of pride in pain.

> "O World! O Life! O Time!
> On whose last steps I climb,
> Trembling at that where I had stood before;
> When will return the glory of your prime?
> No more—oh never more!

MAD SHELLEY

> "Out of the day and night
> A joy has taken flight;
> Fresh spring and summer and winter hoar
> Move my faint heart with grief, but with delight
> No more—oh never more!"

These are words such as a colossal hero of Shakespeare's might have spoken as he toppled to his death—these are words such as the last man on earth might speak, when the idiot's tale is done and when he and all that he has been and the uncountable generations before him have been, stand poised for a last living instant on the rim of silence, signifying nothing. They lie too deep for tears and they stand too erect for pity. Here is tragedy, here is defeat and death, but here too is a majesty that transcends them all and a song that tells us that Samson hath quit himself like Samson, man like man. . . . And that, in the end, was all that mattered. Man and the life of man, to them who sit in space beyond the ends of space and weave the stars into patterns for their amusement, may very well be matters of dubious importance; to us who are ourselves men the case seems a bit different. The perspective is determined by the point of view, and the point of view by the position of the judge in the organic cosmos. Shelley's position was that of Man—so simply, so completely essentialized that he appears to us who see him from a distance less as a reality than as a symbol. He was a pure, clean-stript spirit, passionately alive and aware. Looking at men, he saw them as beings of finite achievement and infinite aspiration, earthbound and circumscribed in actuality, limitless in potentiality. Was it not ridiculously obvious that their one, their only, reason for existence was to heed the spirit that was in them and of them—to play the ape to their dreams? The good fight was the fight of man toward godhead. It was to be fought by the liberated individual with a liberated will. In it lay all the beauty which the universe had to give.

Lover

Shelley was the prophet of mankind's spiritual freedom and the poet of the beauty which was implicit in their quest thereof. Simultaneously he was the leader who rides at the head of an army, directing and exhorting his men, and the bard who stands apart upon some eminence above the field of war, descries the glint of swords and polished armor, the surge of marshalled hosts in conflict, and sings of what he sees. Like Odysseus, he was active, like Homer, contemplative; and in his combined rôle of "doer" and "seer," of hero and hero-maker, he perceived both that life was tough and earnest and that it was beautiful, that the world was no more a pageant of marching armies than a shambles of mangled soldiers—and no less. He saw in mass victory the untold suffering of individuals and in defeat the glorious deeds of single heroes; he discovered in his own life the utter inseparability of triumph and pain in triumph, of disaster and greatness in disaster. Life, like the earth on which it generates, spins on its perhaps predestined course, careless in its means, obscure in its ends—a monstrous chaos of conflicting aspects and warring values, in which nothing is permitted to exist which does not forthwith and with divinely ordered irrationality beget its opposite. The great majority of men, happily secure in their appointed positions in the communal machine, are spared the insane spectacle of the whole of which they are themselves a part: the general in headquarters, the infantryman in the front line, the widow by the tombstone, the historian in his study see the field of battle from distinct points of view and form evaluations which are subjectively valid. Their reactions may not be pleasant, but at least they are sane, for their range of vision is small enough to be intelligible, and their predetermined relationship to the whole is assurance of their rational functioning. The iron moulds in which all human thought is contained are the utterly uncombinable "sets" of the subjective and the objective: the top-sergeant and the historical philosopher cannot by the exertion of any human faculty see war with the same eyes; each living spirit is insulated from every other and from the whole of which he is an organic part by the impenetrable wall of his own identity. Shelley demanded the absolute. Now the poet, now the reformer, at one moment interpreting the world with the aloof contemplation of a philosopher and at the next hurling himself into this or that of its passing currents with the extrovertive zeal of a champion-at-arms, he tore himself completely out of any "setting" which society could be expected to recognize and, in the process, became—to the eyes of those of us who view him from a reasonable distance—less an actual man than a symbol of man's spirit. He was not content to be merely a combatant or merely a spectator, to be philospoher, or reformer, or scientist, or poet, or man of action, or, indeed, anything which can be designated by a name. With the insane confidence of a child he rejected as superficial and unsatisfying all those innumerable, phenomenalized reflexes through which essence manifests itself in form and sought essence itself—the absolute, the prime-mover, the One in which all things have their birth, their being, and their death. He sought God, if you will, but a God who was more than a word. He sought him in the spirit of man. And the spirit of man is Love.

"Thou demandest what is love? It is that powerful attraction towards all that we can conceive, or fear, or hope beyond ourselves, when we find within our own thoughts the chasm of an insufficient void, and seek to awaken in all things that are, a community with what we experience within ourselves. . . . This is the bond and the sanction which connects not only man with man, but with everything that exists." It was also the bond which connected not only Shelley the Prophet with Shelley the Poet, but the complete Shelley with the world. We have said that he believed the prime purpose of man on earth was to close, by however infinitesimal stages, the enormous gap between his actual and his potential self, and that his sole instrument toward this end of self-apotheosis was his own free spirit. The core of that spirit is desire "beyond ourselves"; it is the urge of imperfection toward perfection, of the incomplete toward consummation, and it manifests itself in every natural process of organic nature, no less in the fertilization of the earth by the sun than in that of woman by man. It is the life process, the affirmation of continued, active existence, and without it all things would be either static nonentities or static gods. There can be no life—of which we can well conceive—without energy, no energy without desire, and no desire without incompleteness. All things are dependent upon each other, attract and are attracted by each other, and, though the process be designated in its various manifestations by such dissimilar names as gravity, natural selection, and human love, it is essentially one. No man nor thing nor concept can exist alone. The spirit that moves within each insufficient unit gropes outwards toward other units, combining, recombining, and eternally seeking in blind necessity the complement which will make it whole. In this manner does the life-force, which has diffused itself centrifugally in the infinite diversity of phenomena, exert its counterbalancing centripetal pull; through their incompleteness are all created things impelled toward completeness—all matter toward other matter, all men toward other men, all spirits toward the Spirit, all transient phenomena toward the enduring noumenon that is the perfect One. That is the *furor amantis* as it expressed itself in Shelley.

It is imperative for us of a generation for whom love is an exclusively subcinctural emotion to remember that for Shelley it was not simply a rather elementary physiological reflex, but a highly spiritualized reflex of such intensity that it may be said to be the basic force of his whole nature. It is easy for the fashionably hard-boiled intellect of the twentieth century to show (to its own satisfaction) that he idealized love—as he did everything else with which he came in contact—out of all reality, and that his pseudo-exaltation of a robust, healthily earthy stimulus-response mechanism into a highly nebulous variation of the notorious "cosmic urge" motif is at bottom merely pretentious rot. What the aforementioned fashionably hard-boiled intellect is apt to forget is that his own judgment is not infallible and that there have happened to be some few tolerable intellects in the course of history who have quite sincerely believed that one sound idea is worth a thousand facts and one gorgeously undemonstrable ideal a thousand-thousand glib sophistications. Shelley "idealized the real" for the supremely simple reason that thereby he believed himself to be attaining to a far truer and more absolute reality than was to be found in the confused material phenomena of the world.

NOUMENON

The vast majority even of intelligent men take the material world for real, because they live chiefly through their senses; Shelley believed in the ideal world, because he lived through his intellect. There was no more meaning for him in the bleakly unimaginative orgasm which constitutes the love-consummation as most men know it than there is in the idealized passion of Laon and Cythna for a Jugoslavian muleteer or a B.M.T. subway guard; just as the sexually emancipated young sophisticate who has recently emerged from two chapters of Samuel Schmalhausen and a pamphlet of Margaret Sanger's cannot conceive why sentimental idiots make so much fuss over such a simple procedure, so this sexually emancipated young innocent, who had just turned England's stomach with the nauseous indecencies of his poetry, could on his part not understand how men could deny their most precious birthright and love like beasts when they might love like gods. Shelley himself loved so completely—so universally—that in him the passion grew to well-nigh unrecognizable proportions, became less an attribute of his being than his being itself, less an emotional response to occasional stimuli than a sustained madness of desire. It was love that bound the prophet and the poet in him into perfect unity and that motivated him in every word he ever wrote, every act he ever performed; it was the only standard of value by which he measured the topsyturvydom of the world, the lodestar that he followed in all of his wanderings of the spirit. For him it was the one invincible affirmation which man might pit against the uncounted, uncountable negations which beset his path.

For various rather questionable reasons the name of Shelley has come down to us with the tag of "Platonist" attached. He concurred in many of the Greek philosopher's theories of relationship between the sexes and he was an ardent admirer of the mastery with which he combined thought and poetry in all his writings; but there the affinity ceases. In temperament and attitude they were utterly dissimilar, and, however closely they may have agreed in their notions on the emancipation of women and their advocacy of ideal, ambisexual love, the means whereby they sought this common end were so unlike that those ends themselves become essentially unlike. Plato was a philosopher, and a poet in spite of himself; Shelley a poet, and a philosopher in spite of himself. In their approach toward love, as indeed, toward everything, the one began with the ideal and sought, by purely intellectual processes, to work it into the structure of human society, whereas the other began with the real and brought it to abstraction; whereas Plato worked, rationally, from personal concept toward communality, Shelley proceeded, imaginatively, from society toward the individual. True "platonic love" is the product of a primarily social-minded thinker; it does not spring from the irrationally intuitive spirit whose every desire is inseparable from the "self" from which it generates, but from the objective mind which sees life primarily in its communality; it is not a passionate active force to be used in man's struggle with the cosmos, but a more or less practical means by which the individual may fit himself into harmonious relationship with the whole of which he is a part. Platonism and Shelleyism are alike only in their consecration to the idea and the ideal; in their essential attitude they are as unlike as the civilizations from which they sprang and of which they represent exquisitely refined expressions. The Greek saw society as the working unit, the Englishman saw the individual, and in no aspect does this dissimilarity of attitude better exhibit itself than in their conceptions of love. Love, for Plato, was the essentially static tie which bound man to man to their mutual advantage as members of the community; for Shelley it was the progressively active force by which the incomplete individual might establish contact with the complete and universal One toward which his being aspired. In the last scales, Plato's love is worldly, Shelley's transcendental.

It has often been observed that the greatest spirits among men are those in whom there is the most perfect equilibrium between masculine and feminine elements. There was much that was womanly in Jesus, in Lao-Tse, in Gautama the Buddha, in Goethe and Plato and Shelley, and an unprejudiced mind must admit, in a consideration of these men, that there appears to be an intimate connection between their greatness of soul and their ambisexuality. Humankind is composed of the two dissimilar sexes of man and woman, yet we think of it essentially not as a dual but as a single species, in which its two component parts are not merely complementary, but generically one. The ideal abstraction of Man, as we conceive him in his relation to the absolute, is the hermaphrodite, and the human being in whom we must recognize true universality of spirit must, of necessity, be hermaphroditical to the extent that he represents not merely the male but the female elements which together form the unified concept of "mankind." Shelley was mad for the absolute, and his all-demanding nature could no more be content with being simply masculine or simply feminine than with being simply philosopher, or prophet, or poet. We have tried to point out that the very life-force which animated him was love, and we have seen how different that love was from the passion of normal men. Its difference lay primarily in its comprehensiveness, its comprehensiveness in its androgynous nature. Shelley's love was surely not that of a woman, but neither was it solely that of a man: it was, rather, the love of the idealized human being—the symbolic Man—which incorporated in itself the twin principles of male and female and which, in that incorporation, became the absolute, "complete" human being. To use Hegel's concept, he could never stop either with "thesis" or "antithesis" but must always go on to the "synthesis," in which alone for him there was meaningful reality. To love greatly and comprehensively was not only the prime purpose of his consciousness but the prime need of his unified being. It was not enough to love as a male member of mankind; he must love as mankind itself.

In a recent paper, done in the modern psychological manner, George Barnefield presents much material calculated to prove that Shelley was distinctly bisexual in nature. In the course of his discussion he points to such indications as the romantic affection the young poet felt for men as well as for women, the theme of incest which appears in "Laon and Cythna" and again in "The Cenci," and the perfect being, called Hermaphroditus, which was created by the Witch of Atlas, and concludes therefrom that he was possessed of what the modern post-Freudean jargon calls "a complex." Barnefield's observations are excellent, but his deductions tend to place too much emphasis upon the subconscious and hence to complicate a personality of which the keynote is utter simplicity. The day is not yet in sight when men will know the true relationship between mind and body, between the conscious and the unconscious in the human organism, but it

NOUMENON

is safe to say of Shelley that his component parts were well enough integrated so that he knew at all times pretty much what the various parts of him were about. For those various parts, however unrelated they may appear to the casual observer, were simply the logical reflexes of the single spirit that was in him. His ambisexuality as expressed in any of its many aspects—in his affection for Hogg and Hunt and Dr. Lind, or in his idealization of the brother-sister passion of Laon and Cythna, or in the fascination which hermaphroditical statues exerted upon him—is inevitable when one considers how spontaneously it springs from the "synthetic love" which was the very fabric of his being. It is easy enough for the mechanistic psychologist to say that the cause for behavior is always to be found in some physical stimulus; but is it not more reasonable, in the case of a man who lived most entirely in the spirit, to seek in that spirit itself for the nature of his being rather than in obscure functional processes which have no existence apart from the central unity of his organism? Prefaced with the ready admission that all personality is at bottom an insoluble riddle, it yet does seem nearer to the truth to say that Shelley exhibited androgynous tendencies because he aspired to universal love than that he evolved an ideal of bisexuality because he was a physiological freak.

Platonic love is the abstraction of a philosopher who would have tolerated Shelley in the confines of his utopian state for exactly the length of time that it would have taken to pitch him over the frontier; in his Republic there was no place for the *amator furiosus*, and all the madman's protestations of rational concurrence with his various theories anent homosexuality and the emancipation of women would help him not one whit. He desired men to cultivate love in much the same manner as justice and with a steady eye to its benefits to society—as society existed; he emphatically did not approve of men who were drunk with their visions and who saw in their love a strictly personal relationship between themselves and the absolute, with a fine disregard of the intermediary social machine which was the true entity. And Shelley was so constituted that he would have been not merely a misfit, but a mortal menace, in any society ever organized upon the earth, from Plato's to Lenin's. He was no more a Platonist in spirit than he was a Methodist in intellect, and, whatever affinities of mind there may be said to exist between the poetical philosopher who wrote the "Symposium" and the philosophy-bitten poet who wrote "Laon and Cythna," they are counteracted many times over by the irreconcilable difference in their standard of values. Love, for Plato, was a means to the end of "just" living; for Shelley it was the end itself—the affirmation of continued, progressive life, the blind, unending quest of the incomplete for the complete. The perfect consummation was never to be attained, for in attainment the need for continued love would vanish; the accomplished ideal was no ideal at all. Shelley's whole nature was on-pushing, star-grasping. He could, like Faust, say to the living reality of no passing moment, "Verweile doch, du bist so schön," because he knew that the highest destiny, as the highest happiness, of man lay not in fulfilment but in endless progression toward fulfilment. It is a woful error to assume that, in his yearning for the unattainable, he became incapable of appreciating those approximations to perfection which are vouchsafed to men, and any one who doubts his ability to feel honest, earthly passion should turn to the passage in "The Revolt of Islam" in which he describes the union of his hero-couple and disabuse himself of the notion. Shelley the Lover began his flight with woman, even as Shelley the Prophet began with actual social and political conditions and Shelley the Poet with the sensuous stuff of the material world; but, like them, he could never stop with the phenomenalized "thing," and must always go on to the essence beyond the thing, the universal beyond the individual. And thus it was that in the end the women whom he loved and to whom he sang his song of blind desire were not merely Harriet or Elizabeth or Mary or Emilia or Jane, but Maya, the unattainable, the ineluctable she, "who is all things to all men." Through the real he caught the surmise of the ideal; through the eyes and the bodies and the voices of sundry women he perceived the Woman that he sought. For in his heart he could not but feel that all transitory things were less realities themselves than the symbols of the one ideal reality for which he thirsted; beyond the human women whom he loved—the gay, gallant, lovely women who gave to him their finest moments and with whom he knew the sweetest, happiest hours of his life—there beckoned to him always the "Ewig-Weibliche," the perfect woman-soul that he must ever seek and never find. It was the great quest of Shelley's life. In it there lay all pain and frustration and defeat, but in it too lay all the hope and joy and victory of man. For the quest itself was love.

The quest was love, and he whose life was at bottom an unfaltering consecration to its fulfilment was above all else a lover. We have seen that in the diverse manifestations of the life-force that moved within him he was many things: a child who steadfastly refused to see as his elders bade him see and react as they would have him react, and who, in the face of a world in which conformity is the one rule of life, maintained unsullied the innocent sanctity of his own free self; a prophet of that spiritual liberty through which alone man may be enabled to assert the highest that is in him and through which he may in the end grow from the imperfection of his actuality to the undreamed perfection of his potentiality; a poet, who in his search for the perfect, flawless beauty which all men dream of but which no men know, found the most splendid reflection of it not in the accomplished facts of the material world but in the unaccomplished and never-to-be-accomplished struggle of man against the universe. And finally we have seen a lover, and in seeing him have perhaps approached as close as we may to a knowledge of the united man. For it was love that was at once the need, the purpose, and the substance of his being. It was the sign-post by which his imperfect and incomplete individual identity was directed in its lifelong search for perfect, complete identity in the universal; it was the force through which the spirit that was in him sought to establish a mute communion with all that lay beyond it, in which all men and all things, separate and insufficient in themselves, would attain to the fused sufficiency of oneness; it was the desire which knew not its own end but whose very existence depended upon the non-attainment of that end, in the grip of which he might never rest nor turn aside nor acquiesce, but must always go forward toward the perfect consummation that was godhead. Shelley's love was mystical only in the sense that he recognized man's organic unity with the whole of which he is a part, unworldly only in his complete unwillingness and his complete inability to believe in any abiding reality save that ideal whole. Life, for him, was the consecrated struggle from imperfection to perfection, from actuality to potentiality, and love was the affirmation implicit in that struggle. Its antithesis is not hate, but indifference—the great leaden-eyed indifference of earth that asks no questions and fights no battle and sings no song. It was "die Trägheit des Herzens"—the sloth of the heart—that made the spiritual purity of Caspar Hauser the seal and warrant of his doom; it was the dull and dreamless contentment of men with the great "whatever-is" and their resentment of any who would disturb their sleep that led Jesus Christ to the hill of Golgotha; it was at bottom neither hate nor cruelty nor badness, nor, indeed, any so vitally positive a spirit, but *indifference* that was the cardinal evil of the world. It was against the massed acquiescence of the earth that Shelley flung himself with the fury of a prophet, of a poet, and of a lover, and it was against the enormous negation of death and the visionless acceptance of death that he threw the magnificent affirmation of his spirit and his song. Adonais must die—man must die—but only that thereby he may live in richer, fuller measure and be at last incorporated into the perfection of the abiding whole. "The One remains," and toward that One all things tend. It was in that tendency of the transient toward the eternal, of the incomplete toward completion, of the imperfect toward perfection that Shelley found the significance of life; it was in holy devotion to the dream of consummation that he lived and recognized his reason for living. It was the consecration of the Lover—the consecration without end.

And it is as the Lover, rather than as anything else, that Shelley remains in our memory. A century has removed us far from the actuality of his living self, while the ideality of his significance—perhaps in the end the truer actuality—grows clearer and brighter with the uprolling years. What he once accomplished, or did not accomplish, means little to us now; what he eternally stands for becomes ever more precious and more significant. In the perspective of time the human being with all his limitations and imperfections is lost in the abiding sufficiency of the symbol. The man is dead. The gesture of that man remains: the gesture and the image of one who saw and felt far more than common men—of one who, in the face of a world of evil and ugliness and misery and of a universe wherein was neither rest nor surety nor permanence for men, held fast to an idealism that was not protective but triumphant —of one who suffered and wept and who yet did not bow, who stood upon the earth that was his home and flung into a silence and a void his undying affirmation of liberty and of love and of the dearness of life. With such a gesture and to such an end did Percy Shelley live and sing.

We see him there. We see other men. And again, suddenly, inevitably, we know that he was mad.

EVALUATION

Unity

ALL men—whether in admiration, in condemnation, or in disinterested scrutiny—have perceived that Shelley was "different." From the intimate circle of those who knew him personally down to those of us who know him only vicariously through his creations, from Harriet and Mary and Byron and Trelawney down through Browning and Arnold and Dowden and Maurois and Peck to this particular Princeton student who attempts his evaluation at the distance of a hundred years and three thousand miles there is a record of no single person who has not been possessed of the feeling that he was fashioned of another fabric and animated with another spirit than the normal run of men. Perspective and point of view have made no difference. The family at Field Place, the society of Eton, of Oxford, of contemporary England, and finally posterity at large have all concurred in the judgment that here was a being who was solitary among his fellows; it is the one certainty from which all opposed and contradictory evaluations have had their common beginning and in which, if anywhere, the mainspring of the man's nature must be sought. At the outset we predicated that he was unique. Here, at the conclusion, we must try to place our finger on the reason.

Shelley was a unified personality. Every act he ever performed, every word he ever spoke or wrote bears witness to the integral oneness of his being—a oneness to unprecedented in human nature and so incredibly perfect in its constancy that, by virtue of its very obviousness, it is difficult to see. In an attempted interpretation of the character of any individual the natural direction is away from the superficial simplicity of the whole toward that underlying complexity which we have come to believe is implicit in all character. This is the direction which many critics of Shelley have followed, and in so doing they have made their great mistake. Instead of appealing directly to the animating spirit of the poet they have concentrated their attention upon this or that particular manifestation of that spirit, with the inevitable result that the whole became obscured in the multiple aspects which it offered and which, apart from it, had no proper existence of their own. Thus Jeaffreson has seen him as a hypocritical wretch with a golden voice, Matthew Arnold as "a beautiful and ineffectual angel," Maurois as an Arielesque wanderer from another, brighter planet, Barnefield as a mildly pathological example of bisexuality, Whitehead as a potential organic chemist. He has been called "ethereal," "irresponsible," "selfish," "erratic"; he has been lauded as a poet and damned as a man; and in the end he almost invariably has been pulled into so many parts that the single, indivisible reality of his "self" has well-nigh disappeared. "Ethereal," for example, is an excellent word to apply to much of his verse, "erratic" and "irresponsible" to the impression which he made upon preeminently social-minded people, but to carry these appellations over and establish them as the keynote to his essential character is comparable to calling the sun the size of a nickel because it appears so to our unaided eyes. Shelley was no more erratic than he was illiterate, and the strange, though explicable, paradox is that it is his very constancy of spirit which has produced this impression.

EVALUATION

We call him irresponsible because he seldom behaved in the expected way; what we are apt to forget is that he seldom behaved in the expected way because he steadfastly refused to surrender the perfect consistency of his own nature to the makeshift inconsistency of society. During the whole of his life he made exactly two concessions to the Antichrist of Custom; those were his marriages with Harriet and Mary, in his consent to which he waived his dearest principles for the sake of the women he loved. For the rest, he played the game according to the rules of his own heart, and nothing that either men or gods could do was sufficient ever to make him change or falter or repent. In theory his attitude is perhaps the noblest that any man has ever held; in practice it undeniably resulted in great misery both for himself and for those with whom he came in contact and of whom he expected consecration like his own. The right and wrong of it is a moot question: from the distance of a century we see him as beautiful; from somewhat closer at hand our ancestors saw him not merely as reprehensible, but as positively dangerous. That does not concern us here, for it is not our aim either to justify his "difference" or to condemn it, but simply to interpret it. For, in the end, the eternally significant thing about Shelley is not what he thought or did or wrote, but what he was—not that he was one of the great prophets of his age in the cause of freedom, nor that his worldly life was one protracted tragedy of maladjustment to society, nor even that his song is perhaps the purest and most lofty in the world's literature, but that the living spirit of him, to which all these aspects owe their being and in which they mingle indissolubly, was the most completely homogeneous and most perfectly unified force that has been exhibited in any man. Shelley was an integer. To him, more than to anyone else of whom history tells us, it was granted to "be himself."

"Being oneself" is generally considered one of the more elementary accomplishments; it is not until we study the nature of personality with some care that we discover the elusiveness—one may almost say the non-existence—of identity. Life, for the average man, is neither more nor less than a successive series of adjustments to a successive series of conditions, and, in the process, that entity which is the "self" gradually loses all true significance beneath the vast conglomeration of responses and attitudes into which it has dissolved itself to meet the varying situations which the world presents. Pirandello has endeavored to show again and again that we have only a vicarious identity and that we exist as personalities only in the phenominalized reflexes of each passing moment; each of us is far less a unit than a jumble of loosely correlated units under the more or less continuous surveillance of a single consciousness. A normal person's "self" is, in the process of living, diffused into so many channels and subjected to so many modifications that it ceases almost entirely to possess any save an abstract meaning. One man knows another only by lumping together a dubiously related mass of characteristics under the helpful label of a name and correlating them as best he may into a measure of homogeneity; of his personality, in itself, he knows nothing, because there is nothing there to know. It was otherwise with Shelley, and therein lies the secret of his uniqueness. Whereas other men are complex, he is simple, in that he never permitted his integrity of personality, his "sanctity of soul," to be changed or modified by things outside himself. Except in the cases of his two marriages, there is no record of there ever having been the slightest discrepancy

EVALUATION

between what he believed, what he wrote, and what he did; and he committed no act, of any kind whatsoever, which was not directly referable to the united spirit of prophet, poet, and lover that was his "self." John Doe's life is a sustained attempt to adjust himself to the world of which he is a part, and in the effort he forfeits the reality of his own integral personality; he is formed by living from a simple into a complex organism. Shelley's life, on the other hand, was a sustained attempt to maintain his individuality and to force the world to adjust itself to his ways, because he knew that they were the right ways, and in the effort he forfeited his happiness on earth. He would not make concessions, nor surrender the essential entity of himself to the arbitrary entity of society. His one rule of life was to "be himself"; in its observation he maintained through life the perfect simplicity and the indivisible oneness of spirit, which in a world of makeshifts and adjustments and compromises without end makes him unique among men.

Direction

"I go forward until I am stopped, but I never am stopped." Shelley never was. With the tremendous force of his unified personality he flung himself upon the evil of the world, and, if the world showed little inclination to change its ways, he showed less. He matured and acquired wisdom, he shifted (or, better, enlarged) his campaign against political and social injustice into one in which he recognized the massed negation of the universe as his foe, but the cause in which he fought was precisely the same from beginning to end. His enormous vitality against overwhelming odds was made possible only by his unity of spirit; other men, whose energies are diffused in so many directions, are incapable of *caring* so much for any cause, but he, whose whole being was one and indivisible, was by virtue of that oneness possessed of an almost superhuman intensity of purpose. The machinery of his organism was incredibly simple: with eyes that saw innocently, and not as they were taught to see, he looked at the world and perceived in it both goodness and evil, beauty and ugliness; goodness and beauty are desirable, evil and ugliness undesirable; man's highest duty is to make the world in which he is forced to live into the world of his desire. These were the premises, and Shelley never needed more. The direction of his course being determined—the direction from actuality to potentiality, from imperfection to perfection—the question of faltering or turning aside was the last thing that could enter his insanely logical head. There was no end to the quest to which he gave himself in consecration, but neither was there any end to the spirit that impelled him; every particle of his being strained at the leash of earthly limitations and incompleteness, and in that straining alone he found the meaning and the purpose of life. He was never stopped while he lived, because to stop would have been the same as to die. Normal men have many dreams, but the prospect of fulfilment is always too dubious or too remote to be very seriously considered. Shelley had one dream, and in it he lived his life.

Robert Browning had probably a better understanding of Shelley's significance than any other of his critics, and his appraisal of the man's verse is well worth quoting in part: "I would rather," he writes, "consider Shelley's poetry as a sublime fragmentary essay towards a presenti-

EVALUATION

ment of the correspondency of the universe to Deity, of the natural to the spiritual, and of the actual to the ideal, than I would isolate and separately appraise the worth of many detachable portions which might be acknowledged as utterly perfect in a lower moral point of view, under the mere conditions of art." . . . Under the mere conditions of art. Browning realized that it would never do to judge Shelley merely as an artist and that to consider one of his aspects, however self-sufficient when regarded superficially, apart from the whole to which it organically belongs, was little better than mutilation. By reading one or two of his poems we can tell that he was an imaginative genius; by reading one or two pages of any biography we can tell that he was a misfit; in neither case do we discover anything about the true nature of the most amazing personality of modern times. To see Shelley piecemeal is not to see him at all, and to approach his poetry as something complete in itself is to rob both it and its creator of their true significance. For the man and his work were one, even as the poet and the prophet and the lover, the dreamer and the philosopher and the bolshevik and the scientist in him were one, and neither can be divorced from the other without the resultant disintegration of the whole. Above all else he was a Man, and he sang for no other reason than that it is song which is Man's most noble means of expression. "Poetry," he wrote, "is a sword of lightning, ever unsheathed, which consumes the scabbard that would contain it. . . . Poetry is indeed something divine. It is at once the center and the circumference of all knowledge." One might substitute "the spirit of man" for the word "poetry" in these definitions and their validity would be unimpaired, for the one is simply the emanation of the other. His song was an inseparable part of him; it was the sound of his spirit in motion; it was the center and circumference of knowledge, in that it was the center and circumference of the human spirit. Shelley's verse, like the personality from which it generated, is concentrated to the one end that was the goal of his united being, and its mood is not, like that of most poets, one of diffuse appreciation but of intense desire; indeed, one may say that, whereas the average singer has a range of several loosely related moods, he had but one. He harped eternally upon the same note, seeming to derive a masochistic ecstasy from its unending and unanswered vibration, and when, in his writing, he was unable to match the sustained constancy of his spirit, he considered his verse scarcely poetry at all. So much of his work is fragmentary because he was almost incapable of writing a line which was not an expression of his "self"; on those occasions when the artist in him was unable to keep pace with the man he would either write nothing or mark time in translations and in the composition of objective verses, which, however beautiful in imagery and craftsmanship, he could never regard as more than the playthings of an off-hour. His genuine poetry must spring clean and unwarped from the spiritual travail that was his life; it must possess its perfect homogeneity and its unswerving oneness of direction. He wrote song because he lived a song. What he *was* and what he *did* were utterly one.

Shelley was strongly possessed of the feeling that his living, conscious personality was not so much a force in itself as the medium—the mouthpiece—through which a greater power breathed its being into the world; the cen-

EVALUATION

tury which has elapsed since his death and during the course of which the outline of his image has gradually been discovered in clearer and more comprehensive perspective has rather confirmed than invalidated his intuition. His animating spirit, we feel, was more perfectly coordinated, more clearly stripped of all superfluity than is possible in a normally constituted human being, and the unswerving direction of his path through life is so completely unlike the adaptable zigzag course of the world of men as to seem almost the gesture of a member of another species than ours. . . . Another species, and yet, in a deeper and a more real sense, a symbol of that very Man from whom, in his societal nature, he appeared so vastly different. He was a human being so completely reduced to its elements and so essentialized in its nature that, in the end, we see him scarcely as a human being at all; like Bellerophon and Galahad and Heinrich von Ofterdingen and the great galaxy of those legendary figures of old, he stands forth among men not for what he was in the diffused reflexes of his personality but for what he symbolizes in his totality. Considered in its relationship to its age, his existence seems neither more nor less than a natural phenomenon: he was as logically inevitable a product of the world's spiritual evolution as the French Revolution was of its social development; in him the long march of two centuries reached its culmination and the essence of the third Golden Age manifested itself in its purest form. As Goethe was the fullest and Napoleon the most active so was Shelley the most concentrated individual in this greatest day of individualism. His position is much like that of the topmost man in a tumbler's pyramid: standing, as it were, upon the shoulders of his predecessors, he is the ultimate coping-stone of the edifice in the structure of which they are integral parts. Without them he could not have been what he was, for the simple reason that without foundations and walls there can be no pinnacle; in his final being he was an entity, but it is well to remember that the very existence of that entity would have been impossible had not all circumstances been ripe for its appearance. As Shelley's song was not merely a product of an artist but the emanation of a united individual spirit, so was that united spirit not merely a product but an emanation—an incarnation—of the spirit of his age. He stood at the very crest of a long historical development; his life was coincident with the life of that day, immediately before the crash into the confused diffuseness of the nineteenth century, in which the multitudinous threads that had been spun through the years preceding were caught together into a unity of meaning and of purpose. The whole age tended in one direction—the direction of the actual toward the potential, of reality toward ideality, of "whatever is" toward "whatever may be." For one brief, insane moment the spirit of Man was set free from its numberless shackles of earth and earthly preoccupation, and, in its infinite presumption, it bounded straight up at the stars. Shelley was the singer of its song of quenchless hope, the prophet of the freedom, the poet of the beauty, and the lover of the self-sufficient significance that were implicit in the quest. For in that quest lay the only meaning of his life.

The goal was far to seek, perhaps it was forever unattainable; but that did not matter. The one thing was to go forward until he was stopped. And he was never stopped in life.

EVALUATION

Mad Shelley

> "I can give not what men call love:
> But wilt thou accept not
> The worship the heart lifts above
> And the Heavens reject not,
> The desire of the moth for the star,
> Of the night for the morrow,
> The devotion to something afar
> From the sphere of our sorrow?"

The devotion to something afar.... It was the core and the circumference of Shelley's being, the life-flame of his spirit, and therein lay all that "difference" which separated him, as by a bridgeless void, from the world of men in which he lived but to which he did not belong. The normal individual faces the world; Shelley faced the cosmos, and the power of the vision which was in him was so great that to his eyes, bedazzled by eternity, there were no realities and no ends save the one perfect Reality that was the end of all. His unique consecration would not have been possible without the unified simplicity of his personality, nor his personality without the homogeneous spirit of the age from which it sprang and of which it was an incarnation and a symbol; all circumstances tended toward the generation of a being which, in its supreme expression of militant individualism, was to remain through time as both a warning and a challenge to men. For he was both more and less than human, and the only possible decision as to his ultimate worth must be made by each of us individually and subjectively. To those who see life primarily in its communality and to whom the pragmatic ideal of the greatest good to the greatest number of people is the *summum bonum* of existence, he will appear as the arch-enemy of all that is good and abiding and

MAD SHELLEY

well ordered in civilization; but to those who in their hearts cannot but feel that the animating spirit of a man is of infinitely more importance than his overt deeds, who believe with unshakable, albeit undemonstrable, faith that Christ is greater than Christianity and Napoleon more significant than a hundred battles which Napoleon fought, and who see in the magnificent gesture of a free individual spirit more than adequate compensation for a thousand dull-eyed miseries and a thousand dreamless deaths, he will stand aloof as an eternal reminder of what Man at his purest and loftiest may be. We cannot judge except by the relative standards of our personal attitudes, and the moral problem that is implicit in Shelley can never be resolved to the satisfaction of all. It is as humanly impossible as it is humanly undesirable to refrain from taking sides, but the primary aim of an evaluation—indeed the only aim which can be said to possess more than subjective validity—is that of clear and comprehensive perception. The final significance of Shelley is not to be found in the question of whether *it was well* for him to be what he was, but in the simple fact that he *was* at all, and he remains as an image and a symbol in the memory of men not because he was supremely admirable nor yet because he was supremely reprehensible, but because he was unique. Wiser, broader, greater men than he have lived upon the earth, and wiser, broader, greater men are doubtless waiting to be born. There are spirits who rival him, and there are personalities who equal him. But there is nothing in the world that resembles him.

Shelley was mad. He was mad because he stood alone. He was mad because there existed in him, as in no other man before or since, the united frenzy of prophet, poet,

EVALUATION

and lover. He was mad because he was a straight line in a world of easy curves and aimless angles and because, with an utter disregard of those traditions and adjustments to traditions which men have come to think of as the very fabric of human life and with an adamant refusal ever to be content with compromises and half-measures, he went forward, unstoppably, in consecration to a dream. . . . And when all is said and done, and when the idolator, the apologist, and the iconoclast have had their say and retired, it is his madness that is the abidingly significant thing about him. For the gods to whose universality he aspired, he may well possess little more importance than any other conglomeration of protons and electrons of approximately the same mass; but for men—and especially for us of the twentieth century, who live in acquiescence within the shadow of forces which dominate our lives and of which we have not the least comprehension, whose every word and deed is regulated by a code which we have had no part in making, and who, in the uncoordinated diffuseness of our lives, neither know nor care to know our purpose or our goal—he has grown with the years into the portentous symbol of what the human spirit may be in those brief moments of its pilgrimage when it casts off the sanity of earth and aspires in magnificent madness to the bright and beckoning stars.

Whether in approval or in disapproval, in admiration or in condemnation, Percy Shelley is worth a glance. For we shall not look upon his like again.

INDEX

Adonais, 9, 24, 77, 82
Aestheticism, 41
Age of prose, 47
Age of reason, 18
Alastor, 76

Baroque-romantic school, 24-25, 33
Biographers and critics of Shelley, 7, 18, 20, 23-24, 56, 86-88, 102, 109-110, 114

Cenci, the, 77, 102

Decadent poets, 46
Declaration of Rights, The, 19, 75
Defense of Atheism, A, 62, 74, 80
Defense of Poetry, A, 50

Freedom as watchword, 14-15, 20, 27-29, 38, 50
Free verse, 46
French Revolution, 11, 14-15, 26-27, 35, 37-38, 50

Giants, three: Goethe, Napoleon and Shelley, 16, 34-36, 48, 50
Gothic novel, 21-22, 33

Hellas, 19, 25, 78, 82
Humanitarianism, rational, 16, 18-21, 25, 29, 35
Hymn to Intellectual Beauty, 81

Imagists, 46, 48
Indian Serenade, 9
Individualism, 30, 35, 50

Laon and Cythna, 6, 76, 102, 103, 104

Margaret Nicholson, 74
Mask of Anarchy, The, 78, 81, 82

Near-greats: Hugo, Tolstoi and Wagner, 46-47
Necessity of Atheism, The, 19
Neoclassicism, 17

Oedipus, 78

Pamphleteers and radicals, 14
Peter Bell the Third, 78
Philosophers of escape, 41
Plato, 2-3, 8
Poets of cynicism: Byron and Heine, 46
Poets of escape, 30, 32, 40-44
Prometheus Unbound, 9, 24, 28, 60, 68, 77, 80, 82, 87, 90
Pseudoromanticism, 17, 21-22

Queen Mab, 74-75, 79

Radicals of the eighteenth century, 19-20
Revolt of Islam, The, 76, 80, 82, 104-105
Robust poets, 44-45
Romanticism, 38, 40-44, 54-69
Romanticism, early, 13, 21, 30
Rosicrucianism, 21-22

St. Irvyne or the Rosicrucian, 23, 24
Satirists: Fielding, Swift and Voltaire, 13, 19, 27

Shelley, Percy Bysshe, alone among his contemporaries, 30; ambisexuality, 101-03; as Ariel, 55, 90-91; "a child", 52, 57, 61, 65, 71, 75, 105; child of his age, 52; consecration to fulfillment, 104, 114; constancy of spirit, 60, 116; crusader, 70-71, 73-80, 89-90, 113; an emanation of world spirit, 52; faith in ideal world, 25, 98-99, 105-08; faith in intuitive imagination, 69; faith in perfectability of man, 21, 71, 96-97, 107; fight against indifference, 107; humanist and humanitarian, 31, 86, 89, 92, 94; iconoclast, 61-66, 121; idealization of the real, 84; imagination incarnate, 24; individualist, 78, 119; influences on, 18-20, 22-24, 73-74; innocence of spirit, 66-68, 106, 114; integrity of spirit, 57, 60-63, 65, 67-68, 93, 106, 109-14, 116-17, 119; lack of human touch, 63; love as synthesis, 103-04; love as transcendental, 101; "mad", 5-6, 9, 16, 26, 34, 52, 89, 108, 120-21; his madness of desire, 96-97, 105; mastery of sensuous images, 84; metaphysician, 18, 83, 87; misfit, 6, 56, 59, 65, 67, 111, 115; mysticism, 88-89; on nature, 86-88, 92; oneness of didactic and artistic elements, 81-83; passion for occult, 22-23; perception of duality, 95-96, 114; philosophical poetry, 18, 82-83; his poetry an expression of self, 116; as Prometheus, 44, 91-93; quest for perfection, 115, 118-19; as scientist, 86-87; song of affirmation, 51, 108; symbol of Man, 96, 117; symbol of his age, 30, 50, 117-119; unified personality, 109-119; uniqueness, 8, 10, 52, 54-55, 58, 84, 109, 112, 120; unity of spirit, 114; universality, 30, 101, 121; wooer of Maya, 105

Shelley, Percy Bysshe: biographic data, birth, 57; parents, 7, 57, 64; sisters, 22, 59; early school days, 58; Eton, 6-7, 22, 58-60, 62; Oxford, 7, 62, 63, 72; break with family, 62, 72; Irish crusades, 62, 74, 75, 80; Elizabeth Hitchener, 62, 64, 72; Harriet Westbrook, 9, 62, 63, 64, 68, 72, 73, 75, 80; verdict of Chancery Court; flight from England, 62, 72; Mary Shelley (Mary Godwin) 1, 4, 7, 18, 23, 63, 64, 74; at Geneva, 23; in Wales, 74; in Italian exile 77-79

Shelley, Percy Bysshe: seen in comparisons, with Aristotle and Goethe, 54-55; with Arnold, Tennyson and Wordsworth, 71; with Beethoven, Goethe and Napoleon, 38; with Byron, 32, 33, 34; with Coleridge and Wordsworth, 90; with Coleridge, Keats and Wordsworth, 30-32, 69; with Goethe, 66, 71, 79, 83, 87; with Goethe and Heine, 28; with Goethe and Napoleon, 16, 30, 34-36, 117; with Goethe and Shakespeare, 84; with Caspar Hauser, 67; with Hume, 87; with Kant, 84; with Keats, 31, 71, 83-84, 90, 92; with Newton, 87; with Plato, 99-101, 103-

04; with Shakespeare, 94; with Swinburne, 42
Sturm und Drang, 14

Thinkers of modern civilization, 47
To the Skylark, 77
To the West Wind, 28, 77, 82

Triumph of Life, The, 79-80

Wandering Jew, The, 60, 74
Witch of Atlas, The, 78, 81, 82, 102

Zastrozzi, 23, 24, 60, 74

DATE DUE

#47-0108 Peel Off Pressure Sensitive